Jean-François Mallet

SIMPLISSIME

THE EASIEST

FRENCH

COOKBOOK

IN THE WORLD

hamlyn

This recipe book is the end result of years of experience. It is designed to answer the question I get asked almost every day: "What can I cook tonight?"

It can be a real headache to come up with meals for both children and adults every day, especially when you want to think of something new to cook and can only use the ingredients you have in your fridge or cupboard.

In *Simplissime* I want to share some everyday recipes with you, all of which are quick, easy and designed to suit all tastes. Combining simple flavours and ingredients makes it perfectly possible to cook nice little dishes or even large meals without spending hours doing so.

This book is very easy to follow: 2 to 6 ingredients presented in photos, a few lines of text – then all that's left is to let it cook!

Have a great time in the kitchen and enjoy eating the results!

HOW TO USE THIS BOOK

In this book I am assuming you have:
- **Running water**
- **A cooker**
- **A refrigerator**
- **A frying pan**
- **A cast-iron casserole pan**
- **A knife (very sharp)**
- **Salt and pepper**
- **Oil**

  (If not, maybe now is the time to invest!)

What are the must-have ingredients?

- **Tinned and bottled foods:** tins of tuna and sardines in oil, coconut milk and the essential trio of tomato products: purée, paste and chopped.
- **Herbs:** fresh herbs are unbeatable, so they should be your first choice. In an emergency you can always use frozen or dried herbs (but they're not as good).
- **Oils:** olive oil – always choose extra virgin, easily the best – hazelnut, sesame and walnut oil.
- **Pasta:** do not hesitate to vary the type of pasta suggested in the recipes according to your taste (and what you have in your cupboard).
- **Soy sauce:** preferably the Japanese Kikkoman® type, the one with the green top – it's less salty.

Which techniques should you use?

- **Cooking pasta:** cook in a large saucepan in plenty of boiling salted water. Keep an eye on the cooking time if you like your pasta al dente.
- **Cooking in a bain-marie:** this technique allows you to melt or cook food without burning it. Place the bowl or pan containing the food inside another, larger pan of boiling water and you've got a bain-marie.
- **Marinating:** soaking an ingredient in an aromatic mixture to flavour or tenderise it.
- **Beating egg whites until stiff:** add a pinch of salt to the egg whites and use an electric mixer, gradually increasing the speed. Always beat the whites in the same direction to prevent them from going grainy.

- **Whipping cream:** to do this successfully, the cream and the bowl must be very cold (put the bowl in the freezer for a few minutes just beforehand). Use an electric mixer.
- **Peeling an orange:** remove the peel and the white pith with a knife. Cut off both ends of the orange and gradually remove the peel by sliding the blade of the knife between the peel and the fruit, working from top to bottom.
- **Reducing:** it's best to reduce the quantity of a juice or stock by evaporation over heat (so take off the pan lid), while keeping it on the boil. This process concentrates the flavours and gives a smoother consistency.
- **Zesting a lemon:** there are three ways of zesting a lemon.
  If you are a beginner and you want a very fine zest, use a cheese grater on the peel of the lemon, going over each area just once, without touching the white pith. If you are a professional and you want zest that looks like vermicelli, use a zester. If you are resourceful and you want shavings, use a paring knife.

What equipment should you choose?

- **Electric mixer:** its beaters are perfect for mixing sauces, beating egg whites stiff or whipping cream. It can be replaced with a hand whisk and elbow grease though!
- **Hand blender:** also known as a stick blender, this is used to mix liquids (soups, smoothies, milkshakes, etc.). It's very handy, inexpensive, space-saving, and it also means less washing up, because you can put it directly into your mixture – no need to transfer anything to a bowl.
- **Blender:** more expensive than a hand blender and takes up more space but gives a smoother, creamier result – though more washing up as well, because the liquid to be mixed has to be transferred to the special blender bowl.
- **Multifunctional food processor:** as its name suggests, this is a multipurpose machine. It has various tools for chopping, whisking, slicing, mincing and emulsifying.

Which gas mark?

90°C: Gas mark 3	150°C: Gas mark 5	210°C: Gas mark 7	270°C: Gas mark 9
120°C: Gas mark 4	180°C: Gas mark 6	240°C: Gas mark 8	300°C: Gas mark 10

That's everything you need to know.
All you have to do now is follow the recipes!

PARMESAN CRISPS WITH OREGANO

Parmesan shavings
150 g

Dried oregano
1 teaspoon

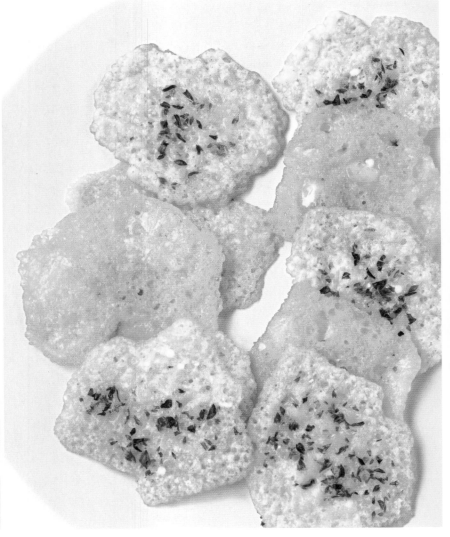

Preparation:
5 minutes
Cooking:
5 minutes

• Place small piles of **Parmesan** shavings in a hot non-stick frying pan.
• When they begin to brown, sprinkle with **oregano**, turn over and cook for a further minute.
• Drain the crisps, put them onto a plate and serve cold with a nice aperitif.

CHEESE PUFFS

Puff pastry
x 1 sheet

Grated cheese
200 g

Preparation:
5 minutes
Cooking:
25 minutes

• Spread the **puff pastry** out onto baking paper and cover the entire surface of it with **grated cheese**. Roll up tightly with the paper and put in the freezer for 20 minutes.

• Preheat the oven to 180°C. Remove the **pastry** from the fridge and open the paper out onto a baking sheet. Cut the **pastry** into slices ½ cm thick and arrange on the baking sheet.

• Bake in the oven for 25 minutes. Serve with an aperitif when hot and golden brown.

PARMESAN AND OLIVE BISCUITS

Black olives
x 20 (stoned)

Parmesan
150 g

Soft butter
100 g

Flour
100 g

Preparation:
25 minutes
Cooking:
15 minutes
Setting:
1 hour

• Chop the **olives** into small pieces and grate the **Parmesan**.
• Using a bowl, mix the soft **butter** with the **Parmesan**, **flour** and chopped **olives** until creamy.
• Arrange the mixture into sausage shapes and leave to set in the refrigerator for 1 hour. Preheat the oven to 180°C.
• Cut each shape into rounds of about 1 cm thick and bake for 15 minutes on a baking sheet.
• Leave to cool before removing from the baking sheet.

MINI SAUSAGE PIZZAS

Rosemary
1 sprig

Pizza dough
1 ball (frozen)

Toulouse sausage
200 g

Lemon
x 1

 Salt, pepper

👪 (x4)

🕐

**Preparation:
15 minutes
Cooking:
25 minutes**

• Preheat the oven to 170°C. Strip the leaves off the **rosemary** and chop. Roll out the **pizza dough** and cut 12 circles of dough with a small pastry cutter.

• Cut the **sausage** into 12 even slices. Arrange the circles of **dough** on a baking sheet, place a slice of **sausage** on each and bake for 25 minutes.

• Remove from the oven, sprinkle with **rosemary** and grated **lemon** peel.

SMOKED SALMON WITH WHIPPED CREAM

Smoked salmon
6 slices

Dill
1 bunch

Whipping cream
330 ml

Lemons
x 2

**Preparation:
10 minutes**

• Cut the **salmon** into small cubes. Wash and chop the **dill** and whip the **cream** in a very cold bowl (put the bowl in the freezer first), using an electric mixer.
• Grate the peel of the **lemons** and squeeze out the juice. Add both the gratings and the juice to the **cream** with the **salmon** and **dill**, and spoon the mixture into ramekins to serve.

12

RICOTTA AND PEA SPREAD

Lemons
x 2

Peas
100 g (fresh or frozen)

Ricotta
250 g

Olive oil
4 tablespoons

Dried oregano
1 tablespoon

Bread
(for the spread)

 **Salt, pepper**

**Preparation:
10 minutes**

• Grate the peel of the **lemons** and squeeze out the juice.
• Plunge the **peas** into boiling water for 2 minutes, drain, then mix with the **ricotta**, **olive oil**, **oregano** and the juice and peel of the **lemons**.
• Season with salt and pepper and serve spread on slices of toast.

CELERY WITH SMOKED SALMON

Celery
4 sticks (small)

Smoked salmon
4 slices

Natural yoghurt
x 2 small pots

Curry powder
1 tablespoon

Olive oil
1 tablespoon

 **Salt, pepper**

**Preparation:
10 minutes**

- Cut the **celery** into small, evenly sized sticks, with or without the leaves.
- Wrap the **celery** sticks in the **smoked salmon**.
- Mix together the **yoghurt**, **curry powder** and **olive oil** in a dipping bowl.
- Season the **salmon** and **celery** sticks with salt and pepper, and serve on a plate with the sauce on the side for dipping.

STUFFED APRICOTS

Apricots
x 16 (firm)

Black pudding
200 g

Preparation:
15 minutes
Cooking:
25 minutes

• Preheat the oven to 180°C. Cut the **apricots** in two and remove the stones.
• Remove the skin from the **black pudding** and mash the flesh with a fork.
• Stuff the bottom halves of the **apricots** with the **black pudding**, place the other halves on top, arrange in an oven dish and bake for 25 minutes.
• Serve very hot with a rocket salad.

18

BAKED ASPARAGUS WITH HAM

Green asparagus
x 20 stems

Dry-cured ham
10 slices

🧂🧂 **Salt, pepper**

👥👥👥👥

🕐

Preparation:
5 minutes
Cooking:
10 minutes

• Preheat the oven to 180°C. Peel and trim the **asparagus**.
• Cut the slices of **ham** in two.
• Wrap each **asparagus** stem in a slice of **ham**.
• Lay out on an oven tray and bake in the oven for 10 minutes.
• Serve warm with mayonnaise on the side.

TUNA SASHIMI WITH WATERMELON

Soy sauce
3 tablespoons

Olive oil
3 tablespoons

Tuna fish
600 g (red or white)

Watermelon
600 g (1 large slice)

**Preparation:
10 minutes**

• Mix the **soy sauce** with the **olive oil**.
• Cut the **tuna** into small, thick slices.
• Remove the skin from the **watermelon** and cut in the same way as the **tuna**.
• Arrange alternate slices of **tuna** and **watermelon** on 4 plates as shown in the photograph.
• Refrigerate. Top with the sauce 2 minutes before serving and enjoy.

CHERRIES WITH BACON

Bacon
10 thin slices

Cherries
x 20

Preparation:
5 minutes
Cooking:
10 minutes

• Preheat the oven to 180°C. Cut the **bacon** slices in two.
• Wash and dry the **cherries**, then roll them up in the **bacon** slices.
• Arrange in an oven dish and bake for 10 minutes. Serve warm with an aperitif.

HOT GAME PÂTÉ WITH BLUEBERRIES

Minced game
300 g

Blueberries
150 g (fresh or frozen)

 Salt

 Pepper

**Preparation:
10 minutes
Cooking:
45 minutes**

• Preheat the oven to 180°C. In a large bowl, mix the **mince** and **blueberries**, season with salt and pepper, then knead together.

• Fill 4 ramekins with the mixture, pressing down firmly, and cook for 45 minutes in a bain-marie.

• Serve hot with a salad on the side.

TERRINE OF DUCK WITH PISTACHIOS

Shelled pistachios
60 g

Duck legs
800 g (about 3)

Sausage meat
200 g

Eggs
x 2

Cognac
4 tablespoons

 Salt

 Pepper

Preparation:
15 minutes
Cooking: 1 hour 15 minutes; Setting: 24 hours

• Preheat the oven to 170°C. Chop the **pistachios** into little pieces. Bone the **duck legs** and chop them in a food processor, then knead together with the other ingredients in a large bowl.

• Press the mixture into a terrine and cook for 1 hour 15 minutes in a bain-marie.

• Refrigerate for 24 hours before serving.

POULTRY LIVER TERRINE

Poultry liver
500 g

Sausage meat
400 g

Eggs
x 2

Thyme
1 teaspoon fresh or dried

 Salt

 Pepper

Preparation:
15 minutes
Cooking: 45 minutes; Setting: 24 hours

• Preheat the oven to 170°C. Cut half the **poultry liver** into pieces and chop the other half in a food processor. Knead all the ingredients together in a large bowl.
• Transfer to a terrine, press down and cook for 45 minutes in a bain-marie.
• Refrigerate overnight and serve cut into nice thick slices.

PORK KNUCKLE TERRINE WITH MUSTARD

Salted pork knuckle
1 kg (cooked on the bone)

Wholegrain mustard
3 tablespoons

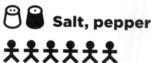 **Salt, pepper**

**Preparation:
15 minutes
Cooking: 10 minutes
Setting: 12 hours**

• Soften the **pork knuckle** in boiling water for 10 minutes.
• Drain, leave to cool, remove the bone and cut the meat with the skin on into small pieces.
• Mix with the **mustard** and then pack the pieces of **pork** into a terrine.
• Refrigerate overnight. Turn out and serve in thick slices with a salad.

CARAMELISED CAULIFLOWER CREAM

Cauliflower
x 1 (900 g)

Butter
100 g

 **Salt, pepper**

👪👤

🕐

**Preparation:
10 minutes
Cooking:
25 minutes**

• Cut the **cauliflower** into small pieces and cook for 20 minutes in a saucepan with just enough water to cover. Drain (reserving the cooking water).

• Melt the **butter** in another saucepan, sear the **cauliflower** in the hot **butter** and brown for a few minutes.

• Add the cooking water, bring to the boil and purée. Season with salt and pepper and serve in a bowl.

GAZPACHO WITH ASPARAGUS

Air-dried ham
4 slices

Green asparagus
x 8 stems

White asparagus
2 large jars (640 g)

Olive oil
2 tablespoons

 **Salt, pepper**

👤👤👤👤

🕐

**Preparation:
10 minutes
Cooking:
15 minutes**

• Preheat the oven to 180°C. Peel and trim the **green asparagus**, arrange with the **ham** in a large oven dish and bake for 10 minutes. Cut all the above into small pieces.

• Using a pan, heat the **white asparagus** in its juice, then purée in a blender.

• Transfer the **white asparagus** mixture onto plates and top with the pieces of **green asparagus** and **ham**, plus a dash of **olive oil**.

CREAM OF CELERIAC WITH SALMON CAVIAR

Celeriac
500 g

Cream
50 ml

Salmon caviar
2 tablespoons

Olive oil
2 tablespoons

 Salt, pepper

**Preparation:
20 minutes
Cooking:
45 minutes**

• Peel and dice the **celeriac** and cook for 35 minutes in boiling salted water.

• Drain off the water, add the **cream** and cook for a further 10 minutes. Season with salt and pepper, purée and leave to cool.

• Serve the **celeriac** in small cups, top with the **salmon caviar**, add a dash of **olive oil** and serve.

CAULIFLOWER SOUP WITH SESAME

Cauliflower
500 g

Cream
1 tablespoon

Sesame seeds
2 teaspoons

Sesame oil
4 teaspoons

Salt, pepper

**Preparation:
15 minutes
Cooking:
40 minutes**

• Cut the **cauliflower** into small pieces, put in a saucepan with just enough water to cover and simmer for 40 minutes over a low heat.

• Purée with a hand mixer, add the **cream** and season with salt and pepper. Serve in individual bowls, with a sprinkle of **sesame seeds** and a dash of **sesame oil**.

COURGETTE GAZPACHO WITH BASIL

Basil
1 bunch

Courgettes
x 4

Pesto
3 teaspoons

Olive oil
6 tablespoons

  Salt, pepper

**Preparation:
10 minutes
Cooking:
30 minutes**

• Wash the **basil** and pick off the leaves. Wash the **courgettes**, cut into small pieces and cook in a pan of water (250 ml) for 30 minutes.

• Add the **pesto, olive oil** and three-quarters of the **basil** leaves. Purée with a hand mixer, season with salt and pepper and leave to cool.

• Add the remaining **basil** and enjoy.

TOMATO AND PEPPER GAZPACHO

Red peppers
x 2

Cucumber
x 1

Olive oil
6 tablespoons

Chopped tomatoes
2 tins (800 g)

Vinegar
4 tablespoons

Cherry tomatoes
200 g

 **Salt, pepper**

👤👤👤👤

🕐

**Preparation:
10 minutes
Cooking:
5 minutes**

• Remove the stalks, seeds and ribs from the **peppers**, then place in a pan of boiling water for 5 minutes.
• Peel the **cucumber**, remove the seeds and cut into cubes. Purée all the ingredients except the **cherry tomatoes** in a blender.
• Season with salt and pepper, cut the **cherry tomatoes** in half and add before serving.

CREAM OF PUMPKIN SOUP WITH HAZELNUTS

Hazelnuts
x 20

Pumpkin
800 g

Cream
200 ml

Hazelnut oil
4 tablespoons

Salt, pepper

**Preparation:
10 minutes
Cooking:
40 minutes**

• Crush the **hazelnuts**. Peel the **pumpkin** and cut the flesh into large cubes.

• Cook the **pumpkin** in a saucepan with just enough water to cover for 35 minutes.

• Add the **cream** and **oil**. Bring to the boil and purée with a hand blender. Season with salt and pepper and serve with the **hazelnuts** and a dash of **hazelnut oil**.

BROCCOLI AND SALMON BROTH

Broccoli
250 g

Rice vermicelli
70 g

Chicken stock
½ cube

Satay sauce
2 tablespoons

Salmon fillets
700 g (skinless)

  **Salt, pepper**

**Preparation:
10 minutes
Cooking:
7 minutes**

- Cut the **broccoli** into small pieces.
- Place all the ingredients except the **salmon** in a large saucepan with 1.2 litres of water. Cook for 5 minutes over a low heat, stirring continuously.
- Cut the **salmon** into cubes, add to the soup and cook for a further 2 minutes.
- Serve in large bowls and eat while very hot.

PRAWN, COCONUT AND CURRY SOUP

Oriental basil
20 leaves

Raw, shell-on prawns
x 20

Rice vermicelli
80 g

Chicken stock
½ cube

Curry powder
2 tablespoons

Coconut milk
1 litre

 Salt, pepper

⏱

**Preparation:
10 minutes
Cooking:
15 minutes**

• Wash and chop the **basil**. Peel the **prawns**.
• Place all the ingredients except the **basil** and **vermicelli** in a casserole dish with 600 ml water. Simmer over low heat for 15 minutes.
• Add the **basil** and **vermicelli**. Leave to rest for 5 minutes, mix and serve.

CHICKEN AND COURGETTE SOUP

Basil
20 leaves

Courgettes
x 2

Spring onions
x 2

Chicken breasts
x 4

Chicken stock
½ cube

 **Salt, pepper**

**Preparation:
10 minutes
Cooking:
20 minutes**

• Wash and chop the **basil**. Trim the **courgettes** and **spring onions** and slice thinly.

• Cut the **chicken** into pieces. Place all the ingredients except the **basil** in a casserole pan with 1.2 litres of water. Simmer for 20 minutes over a low heat.

• Add the **basil**. Leave to rest for 5 minutes, stir thoroughly and serve.

BEEF AND MUSTARD SOUP

Cherry tomatoes
x 20

Minced beef
300 g

Chicken stock
½ cube

Dijon mustard
1 tablespoon

Dried thyme
2 teaspoons

Pasta shells
80 g

 **Salt, pepper**

Preparation:
10 minutes
Cooking:
20 minutes

• Wash the **cherry tomatoes** and cut each one in two. Mould the **beef** into little balls.
• Place all the ingredients except the meatballs in a casserole pan with 1.2 litres of water. Cook for 20 minutes over high heat, stirring occasionally.
• Add the meatballs. Leave to rest for 5 minutes, stir and serve.

GOATS' CHEESE ON A CRUNCHY SALAD

Green asparagus
x 20 stems

Green beans
400 g

Goats' cheese
x 4 discs

Baguette
8 slices

Liquid honey
2 tablespoons

Cider vinegar
2 tablespoons

 **Salt, pepper**

👤👤👤👤

🕐

Preparation:
15 minutes
Cooking:
20 minutes

• Preheat the oven to 180°C. Trim and cook the **asparagus** and **green beans** for 3 to 6 minutes in boiling salted water.

• Cut each **cheese** disc in two and arrange on the slices of **bread** in an oven dish, pour over the **honey** and bake for 10 minutes.

• Arrange the **asparagus** and **green beans** on a serving dish, add the hot cheese toasts, flavour with the **vinegar** and serve.

ASPARAGUS, PARMESAN AND EGGS

Green asparagus
x 20

Olive oil
4 tablespoons

Oranges
x 2

Eggs
x 4

Parmesan shavings
150 g

 **Salt, pepper**

**Preparation:
15 minutes
Cooking:
10 minutes**

• Peel the **asparagus** and cook for 5 minutes in boiling salted water. Grate the peel of the **oranges**, squeeze out the juice and mix with the **olive oil**.

• Boil the **eggs** for exactly 5 minutes. Rinse in cold water and peel.

• Arrange the **asparagus** on a serving dish and place the **eggs** on top. Cover with **orange** sauce and **Parmesan** shavings and season with salt and pepper.

BEAN SALAD WITH PESTO

Broad beans
1 kg

Red onions
x 2 (small)

Pesto
2 tablespoons

Olive oil
4 tablespoons

Pouring cream
2 tablespoons

Basil
8 leaves

 Salt, pepper

**Preparation:
10 minutes
Cooking:
30 minutes**

• Shell the **beans**. Cook in boiling water for 30 minutes and leave to cool in the cooking water.
• Peel the **onions** and slice thinly.
• Drain the **beans** and mix with the **pesto, basil, onions, olive oil** and **cream**. Season well with salt and pepper and serve.

MELON WITH SMOKED SALMON AND MINT

Melon
x 1

Smoked salmon
4 slices

Mint
4 sprigs

Olive oil
6 tablespoons

Lime
½

 **Salt, pepper**

**Preparation:
10 minutes**

• Cut the **melon** into cubes, dice the **salmon**, pick off and chop the **mint** leaves.
• Mix the **salmon** and **mint** with the **melon**.
• Add the **olive oil** and the juice of the **lime**. Season with salt and pepper.
• Mix together, set aside for 2 minutes and serve.

MELON, TOMATO AND BASIL SALAD

Melon
x 1

Cherry tomatoes
x 20

Olive oil
4 tablespoons

Basil
20 leaves

Dried oregano
1 teaspoon

 **Salt, pepper**

**Preparation:
5 minutes**

• Cut the **melon** into cubes and the **tomatoes** in two.
• Mix with the **olive oil**, **basil leaves** and **oregano**, season with salt and pepper and serve in a large dish.

AVOCADOS WITH SMOKED SALMON

Smoked salmon
4 thick slices

Dill
4 sprigs

Limes
x 2

Olive oil
4 tablespoons

Avocados
x 4 (fully ripe)

Chives
1 bunch

Salt, pepper

**Preparation:
10 minutes**

• Dice the **smoked salmon**, chop the **dill** and **chives** and squeeze the **limes**. Mix all these with the **olive oil** in a salad bowl and season with salt and pepper.
• Cut open the **avocados**, remove the stones, fill with the **smoked salmon** and serve immediately.

LENTIL, SALMON AND TARRAGON SALAD

Green lentils
200 g

Salmon steaks
2 x 200 g (skinless)

Tarragon
8 sprigs

Wholegrain mustard
1 tablespoon

Olive oil
4 tablespoons

 **Salt, pepper**

**Preparation:
5 minutes
Cooking:
25 minutes**

- Cook the **lentils** for 20 minutes in a large quantity of water.
- Add the **salmon** and cook for a further 5 minutes without stirring. Drain the **salmon** and **lentils** and leave to cool.
- Wash and chop the **tarragon**.
- Cut up the **salmon** and mix thoroughly with the **lentils** and all the other ingredients. Season well with salt and pepper and serve.

TABBOULEH WITH SALMON AND RADISHES

Pink radishes
x 8

Mint
20 leaves

Lemons
x 2

Salmon steaks
2 x 200 g (skinless)

Fine semolina
4 tablespoons

Olive oil
4 tablespoons

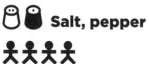 **Salt, pepper**

**Preparation:
10 minutes
Setting:
25 minutes**

• Wash the **radishes** and slice them thinly.
• Wash and chop the **mint**, squeeze the **lemons** to extract the juice and cut the **salmon** into small cubes.
• Mix together the **semolina**, **radishes**, **salmon**, **mint**, **lemon** juice and **olive oil** and season with salt and pepper. Leave to swell for 25 minutes in the refrigerator and serve cold.

ROAST BEEF AND BASIL SALAD

Basil
1 bunch

Cucumber

Roast beef
400 g

Olive oil
2 tablespoons

Soy sauce
1 tablespoon

 Pepper

**Preparation:
15 minutes**

• Wash the **basil** and pick off the leaves. Cut the **cucumber** into thin slices.

• Cut the **roast beef** into thin slices and mix with the **cucumber** and **basil**.

• Add the **olive oil** and **soy sauce** and serve.

66

THAI SALAD

Coriander
1 bunch

Beef carpaccio
400 g (about 4 portions)

Sesame seeds
2 tablespoons

Limes
x 2

Soy sauce
4 tablespoons

Green chilli
x 1 (small)

Preparation:
10 minutes
Cooking:
1 minute

• Wash and chop the **coriander** and the **chilli** and squeeze the **limes**. Sear the **beef carpaccio** for 1 minute in a frying pan with 1 tablespoon of oil, turn off the heat and leave to cool.

• Add the **sesame seeds, lime juice, coriander, soy sauce** and **chilli**. Mix together and serve with rice.

ROQUEFORT SALAD

Shallots
x 4 (large)

Flour
100 g

Little gem lettuces
x 4

Roquefort
150 g

Walnut oil
8 tablespoons

Cider vinegar
4 tablespoons

 **Salt, pepper
+ oil for frying**

**Preparation:
20 minutes
Cooking:
5 minutes**

- Peel the **shallots**, slice thinly and toss in the **flour**. Deep fry and set aside.
- Cut the **lettuces** into quarters and cut the **Roquefort** into small pieces.
- Mix all the ingredients in a salad bowl with the **oil** and **vinegar**. Season with salt and pepper and serve.

CHICKEN LIVER SALAD WITH APRICOTS

Apricots
x 8

Chicken livers
x 8

Rocket
2 handfuls (80 g)

Olive oil
4 tablespoons

Balsamic vinegar
2 tablespoons

Salt, pepper

👤👤👤👤

🕐
**Preparation:
10 minutes
Cooking:
2 minutes**

• Cut open the **apricots** and remove the stones, cut the **chicken livers** into two, wash the **rocket** and shake dry.
• Heat the **oil** in a large frying pan, sear the **livers** for 1 minute, turn, then add the **apricots** and **vinegar** and cook for a further minute. Arrange on the **rocket**, sprinkle with **balsamic vinegar** and serve immediately.

HAZELNUT AND RADICCHIO FARFALLE

Broccoli
100 g

Radicchio
150 g

Hazelnuts
x 20

Olive oil
4 tablespoons

Farfalle pasta
300 g

Parmesan
100 g

 **Salt, pepper**

**Preparation:
15 minutes
Cooking:
20 minutes**

• Cut the **broccoli** into pieces, slice the **radicchio** thinly, chop the **hazelnuts** and fry all these gently in a frying pan with the **olive oil**. Cook for 10 minutes over a low heat. Cook the **farfalle** (al dente) in boiling salted water.
• Drain the **farfalle**, reserving the cooking water, and transfer to the pan. Add 1 tablespoon of the cooking water, the grated **Parmesan** and the vegetables, season with salt and pepper and heat for 5 minutes. Serve.

FARFALLE WITH GREEN VEGETABLES

Courgette
x 1

Green asparagus
x 10 stems

Peas
200 g (fresh or frozen)

Olive oil
4 tablespoons

Farfalle pasta
300 g

Chives
1 bunch

 Salt, pepper

🕐

**Preparation:
15 minutes
Cooking:
20 minutes**

• Cut the **courgette** into rounds. Peel the **asparagus** and cut each stem in two. Fry all the vegetables for 10 minutes in a frying pan with the **olive oil**.

• Cook the **farfalle** (al dente) in boiling salted water. Drain, reserving the cooking water, and transfer to the frying pan. Add 1 tablespoon of the cooking water and the chopped **chives**. Heat for 5 minutes, stirring continuously, and serve with Parmesan.

FUSILLI WITH SARDINES

Mandarins
x 2

Pine nuts
30 g

Fusilli pasta
300 g

Sardines in olive oil
x 2 tins

Raisins
30 g

 **Salt, pepper**

**Preparation:
10 minutes
Cooking:
15 minutes**

- Peel the **mandarins** and cut into pieces.
- Toast the **pine nuts** in a dry pan until golden brown. Cook the **pasta** (al dente) in boiling salted water.
- Drain, reserving the cooking water, and transfer to the frying pan. Add 2 tablespoons of cooking water, the **sardines** and their oil, the **raisins** and the **mandarins**.
- Heat, stirring continuously, and sprinkle with **pine nuts**.

MACARONI CHEESE WITH HAM

Macaroni pasta
300 g

Ham
250 g

Grated cheese
150 g

Cream
400 ml

 Salt, pepper

**Preparation:
5 minutes
Cooking:
45 minutes**

• Preheat the oven to 180°C. Cook the **macaroni** (al dente) in boiling salted water. Drain and transfer to a gratin dish.

• Cut the **ham** into small pieces, then add it to the **grated cheese** and the **cream**. Season with salt and pepper, mix everything together and bake in the oven for 35 minutes. When the crust is nicely browned, serve hot with a green salad.

RIGATONI ARRABBIATA WITH AUBERGINE

Aubergine
x 1 (large)

Olive oil
4 tablespoons

Chorizo
8 slices

Dried oregano
2 tablespoons

Rigatoni
300 g

 **Salt, pepper**

**Preparation:
10 minutes
Cooking:
20 minutes**

• Cut the **aubergine** into pieces and sear in a frying pan with the **olive oil**. Add the **chorizo** and **oregano** and brown for 20 minutes, stirring regularly.

• Cook the **rigatoni** (al dente) in boiling salted water. Drain, reserving the cooking water and transfer to the frying pan, adding 1 tablespoon of cooking water. Heat for 5 minutes and season with salt and pepper.

RIGATONI WITH DUCK CONFIT

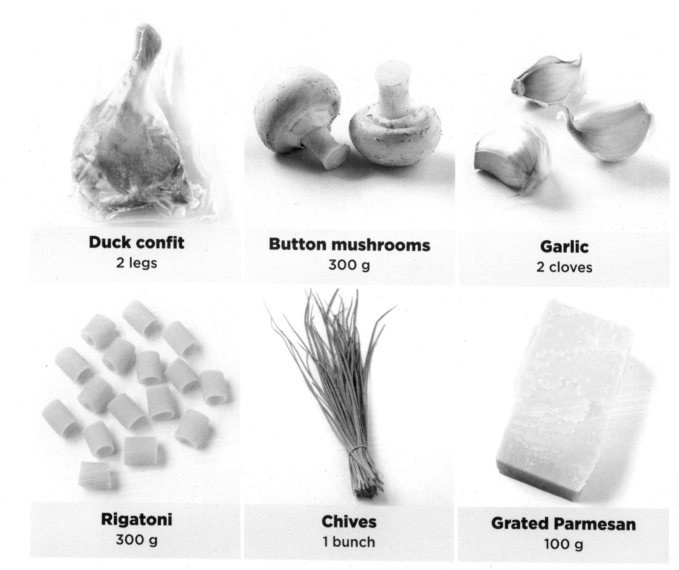

Duck confit
2 legs

Button mushrooms
300 g

Garlic
2 cloves

Rigatoni
300 g

Chives
1 bunch

Grated Parmesan
100 g

 **Salt, pepper**

**Preparation:
10 minutes
Cooking:
25 minutes**

• Chop the **duck** meat with the skin on, slice the **mushrooms** thinly and chop the **garlic**. Fry all these in a pan for 10 minutes.
• Cook the **rigatoni** (al dente) in boiling salted water. Drain, reserving the cooking water, and add to the pan. Add 1 tablespoon of cooking water, the **Parmesan** and the chopped **chives**. Fry for 2 minutes, stirring continuously. Serve in a large dish.

84

PENNE WITH RED MULLET

Olive oil
4 tablespoons

Red onions
x 2

Mullet fillets
x 4 (fresh or frozen)

Dried oregano
1 tablespoon

Penne pasta
300 g

 **Salt, pepper**

**Preparation:
15 minutes
Cooking:
20 minutes**

• Peel the **onions** and slice them thinly. Heat the **oil** in a frying pan, sear the **onions** and brown for 2 minutes, add the **mullet** and **oregano** and cook for a further 10 minutes, stirring regularly.

• Cook the **penne** (al dente) in boiling salted water. Drain, reserving the cooking water, and add to the frying pan with 2 tablespoons of cooking water.

• Heat, stirring continuously. Serve flavoured well with black pepper.

PENNE WITH PUMPKIN AND WALNUTS

Pumpkin
1 slice (about 400 g)

Walnut oil
4 tablespoons

Penne pasta
400 g

Walnuts
10 shelled halves

Parmesan
100 g

 **Salt, pepper**

**Preparation:
5 minutes
Cooking:
45 minutes**

• Preheat the oven to 180°C. Bake the **pumpkin** for 35 minutes with 2 tablespoons of **walnut oil**.
• Cook the **penne** (al dente). Crush the cooked **pumpkin** with a fork. Chop the **walnuts**.
• Mix the **pumpkin**, 2 tablespoons of **walnut oil**, the **penne** pasta and the **walnuts** in a frying pan and heat for 3 minutes. Season with salt and pepper, add the grated **Parmesan** and serve.

PENNE WITH PEPPERS AND BASIL

Red peppers
x 2

Garlic
4 cloves

Penne pasta
300 g

Parmesan
100 g

Basil
30 leaves

  Salt, pepper

♁♁♁♁

🕐

Preparation:
20 minutes
Cooking:
40 minutes

• Cut the **peppers** into pieces, peel and chop the **garlic**, then cook them together for 25 minutes in a saucepan with 300 ml water. Purée with a hand blender.
• Cook the **penne** (al dente) in boiling salted water. Drain and add to the pan with the sauce, add the grated **Parmesan** and most of the **basil**, season with salt and pepper and heat for 5 minutes, stirring continuously. Serve sprinkled with extra basil leaves, if desired.

SPAGHETTI WITH COCKLES

Cockles
1.5 litres

Olive oil
4 tablespoons

Garlic
4 cloves

Flat-leaf parsley
8 sprigs

Spaghetti
300 g

 **Salt, pepper**

👤👤👤👤

Preparation:
15 minutes
Cooking:
25 minutes

• Open the **cockles** in a large frying pan, and add the **olive oil**, chopped **garlic** and chopped **parsley**.
• Cook the **spaghetti** (al dente) in boiling salted water.
• Drain and add to the pan with the **cockles**, cook for a further 5 minutes, stirring continuously, season with salt and pepper and serve.

SPAGHETTI WITH ASPARAGUS AND ORANGE

Green asparagus
x 10 stems

Orange
x 1

Olive oil
4 tablespoons

Spaghetti
300 g

Grated Parmesan
100 g

  **Salt, pepper**

**Preparation:
10 minutes
Cooking:
15 minutes**

• Trim the **asparagus** and cut each stem into two.
• Peel the **orange** and cut into small pieces. Sear the **asparagus** for 10 minutes in a frying pan along with the **olive oil**.
• Cook the **spaghetti** (al dente) in boiling salted water. Drain and add to the pan with the **Parmesan** and **orange**. Heat for 5 minutes, stirring continuously, and season with salt and pepper.

BOLOGNESE WITH CHERRY TOMATOES

Spaghetti
300 g

Olive oil
2 tablespoons

Sweet onions
x 2

Minced beef
400 g

Cherry tomatoes
250 g

Basil
20 leaves

 **Salt, pepper**

Preparation:
10 minutes
Cooking:
45 minutes

• Cook the **spaghetti** (al dente) in boiling salted water and drain.

• Slice the **onions** thinly and brown lightly in a casserole in hot **olive oil**.

• Add the chopped **cherry tomatoes** and 500 ml water and simmer for 30 minutes over low heat. Add the **minced beef**, **spaghetti** and **basil**, cook for a further 5 minutes and serve with grated Parmesan.

SPAGHETTI CARBONARA WITH CRAB

Coriander
1 bunch

Spaghetti
300 g

Eggs
x 2

Cream
250 ml

Curry powder
1 tablespoon

Crab meat
2 tins

 Salt, pepper

👤👤👤👤

🕐

Preparation:
15 minutes
Cooking:
25 minutes

• Wash and chop the **coriander**. Cook the **spaghetti** (al dente) in boiling salted water. Beat the **egg yolks** together with the **cream**, **curry powder** and **crab meat**.
• Drain the **spaghetti** and transfer to a frying pan. Add the **cream** and mix vigorously for 2 minutes over a high heat to thicken. Add the **coriander** and season with salt and pepper.

RISOTTO WITH TOMATOES

Arborio rice
400 g (risotto rice)

Stock
½ litre

Dry white wine
1 glass (150 ml)

Olive oil
6 tablespoons

Cherry tomatoes
250 g

Parmesan
100 g

 Salt, pepper

🕐

**Preparation:
5 minutes
Cooking:
25 minutes**

• Chop the **tomatoes** in half. Place the **rice, stock, white wine,** half the **olive oil** and the halved **tomatoes** in a casserole dish.

• Simmer over a low heat, stirring continuously with a spatula, until the **stock** has been absorbed. The **rice** should still be fairly firm.

• Add the grated **Parmesan** and the remaining **oil** and mix vigorously to thicken. Serve hot with a sprinkling of salt and pepper.

RISOTTO WITH SAFFRON

Arborio rice
400 g (risotto rice)

Stock
½ litre

Dry white wine
1 glass (150 ml)

Olive oil
6 tablespoons

Saffron
15 threads

Parmesan
100 g

 **Salt, pepper**

👤👤👤👤

🕐

**Preparation:
5 minutes
Cooking time:
25 minutes**

• Put the **rice**, **stock**, **white wine**, half the **olive oil** and the **saffron** in a casserole. Simmer over low heat, stirring with a spatula, until the **stock** has been absorbed. The **rice** should still be fairly firm.

• Add the grated **Parmesan** and the remaining **oil**, mix vigorously to thicken.

• Serve with a sprinkling of pepper.

FRIED RICE WITH PRAWNS AND PORK

Shell-on prawns
x 8

Pork ribs (back)
x 2

Fresh ginger
80 g

Soy sauce
8 tablespoons

Curry powder
2 tablespoons

Boiled rice
400 g

Pepper

👤👤👤👤

🕑

**Preparation:
20 minutes
Cooking:
25 minutes**

• Shell the **prawns**, cut the **pork** into small, bite-sized pieces and sear in a wok with 4 tablespoons of oil.
• Peel and grate the **ginger** and add to the wok with the **prawns**, **rice**, **curry powder** and **soy sauce**. Fry over a high heat, stirring occasionally, until the **rice** is well-browned and crunchy. Salt lightly, add pepper and serve.

BUTTON MUSHROOM PIZZAS

Pizza dough
2 balls (frozen)

Double cream
8 tablespoons

Baby spinach
200 g

Button mushrooms
x 16 (large)

Preserved lemons
x 4

Olive oil
8 tablespoons

 **Salt, pepper**

Preparation:
15 minutes
Cooking:
25 minutes

• Preheat the oven to 220°C. Slice the **mushrooms** thinly and dice the **lemons**. Stretch out the **pizza dough** on a baking sheet.

• Top with the **cream**, half the **spinach** and **mushrooms** and the **lemons**. Bake in the oven for 25 minutes. Remove from the oven, add the remaining **spinach** and **mushrooms**, drizzle with **olive oil**, season with salt and pepper and serve.

SPICY PIZZAS WITH PEPPERS

Pizza dough
2 balls (frozen)

Red peppers
x 4

Chorizo
16 large slices

Mint
4 sprigs

Olive oil
8 tablespoons

 **Salt, pepper**

👤👤👤👤

🕐

**Preparation:
15 minutes
Cooking:
25 minutes**

• Preheat the oven to 220°C. Slice the **peppers** thinly. Stretch out the **pizza dough** on a baking sheet and top with the **peppers** and **chorizo**.

• Bake in the oven for 25 minutes. Remove from the oven, add the **mint** leaves, drizzle with **olive oil**, season with salt and pepper and serve.

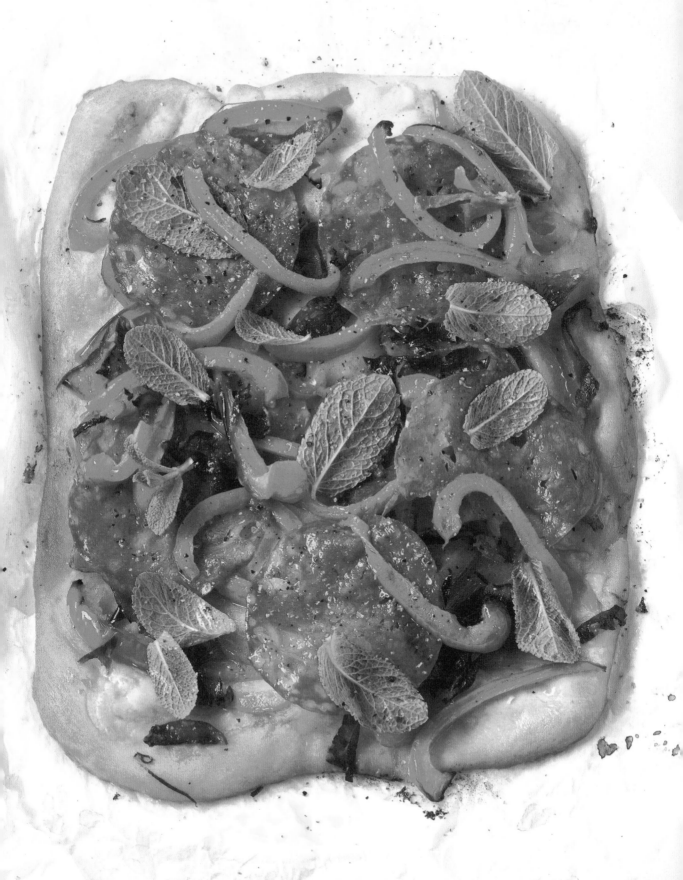

TOMATO AND CHERRY PIZZAS

Pizza dough
2 balls (frozen)

Tapenade
2 tablespoons

Cherry tomatoes
x 24

Sour cherries
40 (frozen)

Basque cheese
100 g (Etorki® type)

Olive oil
2 tablespoons

 Salt, pepper

⏱

**Preparation:
15 minutes
Cooking:
25 minutes**

• Preheat the oven to 220°C. Stretch out the **pizza dough** on a large baking sheet. Cut the **cherry tomatoes** in half.

• Spread with **tapenade** and top with the halved **cherry tomatoes** and the **cherries**.

• Sprinkle with the grated **Basque cheese** and bake in the oven for 25 minutes. Remove from the oven, season with salt and pepper, drizzle with **olive oil** and serve.

GOATS' CHEESE AND THYME CALZONES

Pizza dough
2 balls (frozen)

Goats' cheese
x 4 discs

Tomatoes
x 2 (medium)

Olive oil
4 tablespoons

Thyme
4 sprigs

 Salt, pepper

**Preparation:
15 minutes
Cooking:
25 minutes**

• Pre-heat the oven to 220°C. Form the **pizza dough** into 4 balls and stretch out. Slice up the tomatoes.
• Place 1 **goats' cheese** disc and ½ a **tomato** slice in the centre of each.
• Season with salt and pepper, add 2 tablespoons of **olive oil** and **thyme** leaves and close up your dough to form calzones.
• Press the edges together with your fingers and bake in the oven for 25 minutes. Remove from the oven, leave to rest for 5 minutes, then serve with a salad.

HAM, DANDELION AND PEAR PIZZAS

Pizza dough
2 balls (frozen)

Cream
4 tablespoons

Air-dried ham
8 thin slices

Dandelion leaves
200 g

Pears
x 2

Olive oil
2 tablespoons

 **Salt, pepper**

**Preparation:
15 minutes
Cooking:
25 minutes**

• Preheat the oven to 220°C. Chop the **ham** into small pieces. Stretch out the **pizza dough** on a large baking sheet. Top with **cream** and chopped **ham**.

• Bake in the oven for 25 minutes. Remove from the oven, add the **dandelion leaves** and thin slices of **pear**, drizzle with **olive oil**, season with salt and pepper and serve.

COURGETTE AND HAM PIZZAS WITH PESTO

Pizza dough
2 balls (frozen)

Pesto
2 tablespoons

Courgettes
x 2

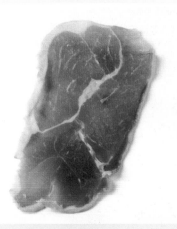

Air-dried ham
8 slices

Olive oil
4 tablespoons

  **Salt, pepper**

**Preparation:
15 minutes
Cooking:
25 minutes**

• Preheat the oven to 220°C. Stretch out the **pizza dough** on a large baking sheet.

• Spread with **pesto** and top with **ham** and thin slices of **courgette** cut with a vegetable peeler.

• Drizzle with **olive oil**, season with salt and pepper and bake in the oven for 25 minutes. Remove from the oven and serve.

116

DUCK AND DATE PIE

Dates
x 10

Sausage meat
50 g

Cognac
50 ml

Duck confit
4 legs

Puff pastry
x 2 sheets

 **Salt, pepper**

👤👤👤👤

🕐

**Preparation:
15 minutes
Cooking:
40 minutes**

• Preheat the oven to 180°C. Cut the **dates** and **duck** flesh into small pieces and mix with the **sausage meat** and **cognac**.

• Spread out one sheet of **puff pastry** on a baking sheet. Place the filling in the centre, cover with the second sheet of pastry and press the edges together. Bake in the oven for 40 minutes. Serve hot with a salad.

LEEK AND PARMESAN TART

Leeks
x 5 (small)

Puff pastry
x 1 sheet

Parmesan shavings
100 g

Double cream
2 tablespoons

Olive oil
2 tablespoons

 **Salt, pepper**

**Preparation:
15 minutes
Cooking:
40 minutes**

• Preheat the oven to 180°C. Trim the **leeks**, cut in half lengthways and wash in plenty of water.
• Line a flan dish with the **pastry**, add the **leeks** and cover with **Parmesan, cream** and **olive oil**.
• Season with salt and pepper and bake in the oven for 40 minutes. Serve hot with a green salad.

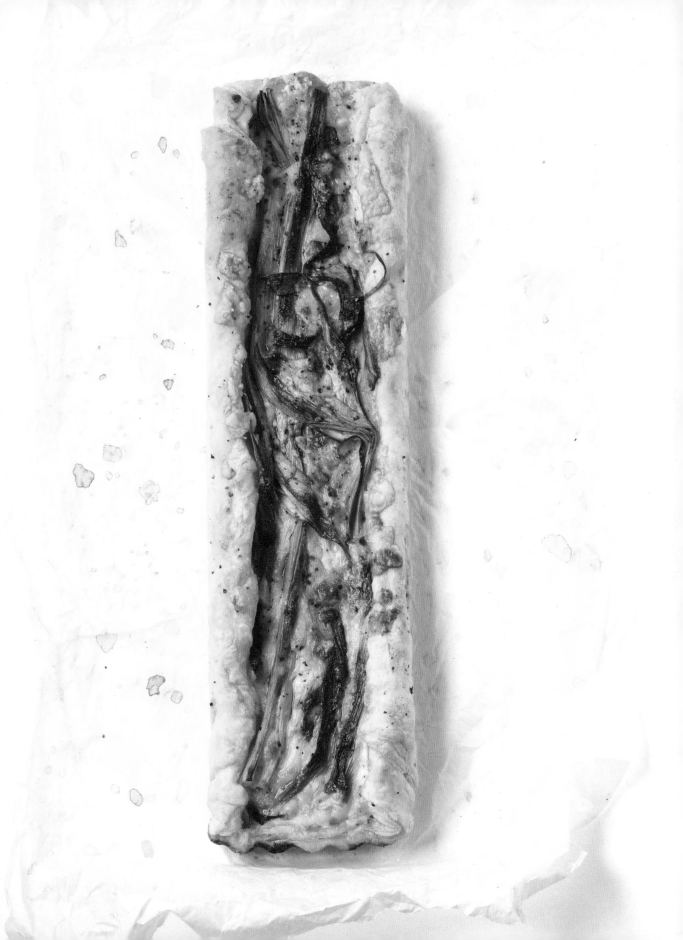

CHERRY TOMATO AND MUSTARD TARTLETS

Puff pastry
x 1 sheet

Dijon mustard
4 tablespoons

Cherry tomatoes
x 32

Olive oil
4 tablespoons

Thyme
4 sprigs

 Salt, pepper

👤👤👤👤

🕐

**Preparation:
10 minutes
Cooking:
35 minutes**

• Preheat the oven to 180°C. Cut 4 circles of **pastry** using a tartlet tin as a pastry cutter.
• Place the **pastry** circles in the tins, top each with a tablespoon of **mustard**, 8 **cherry tomatoes** cut in half and 1 tablespoon of **olive oil**.
• Sprinkle with **thyme leaves**, season with salt and pepper and bake in the oven for 35 minutes. Serve hot or cold.

SMOKED SALMON AND APPLE TARTS

| Pizza dough | Ricotta | Smoked salmon |
| 2 balls (frozen) | 250 g | 4 slices |

| Green apples | Chives | Lemon |
| x 2 | 1 bunch | x 1 |

 **Salt, pepper**

👤👤👤👤

🕐
**Preparation:
15 minutes
Cooking:
25 minutes**

• Preheat the oven to 220°C. Stretch out 4 rounds of **pizza dough** on a large baking sheet, top with **ricotta** and bake in the oven for 25 minutes. Cut the **apples** into batons and chop the **salmon** and **chives**.

• Remove from the oven and top with the **salmon**, **apple** and **chives**. Drizzle with **lemon juice**. Season with salt and pepper and serve.

124

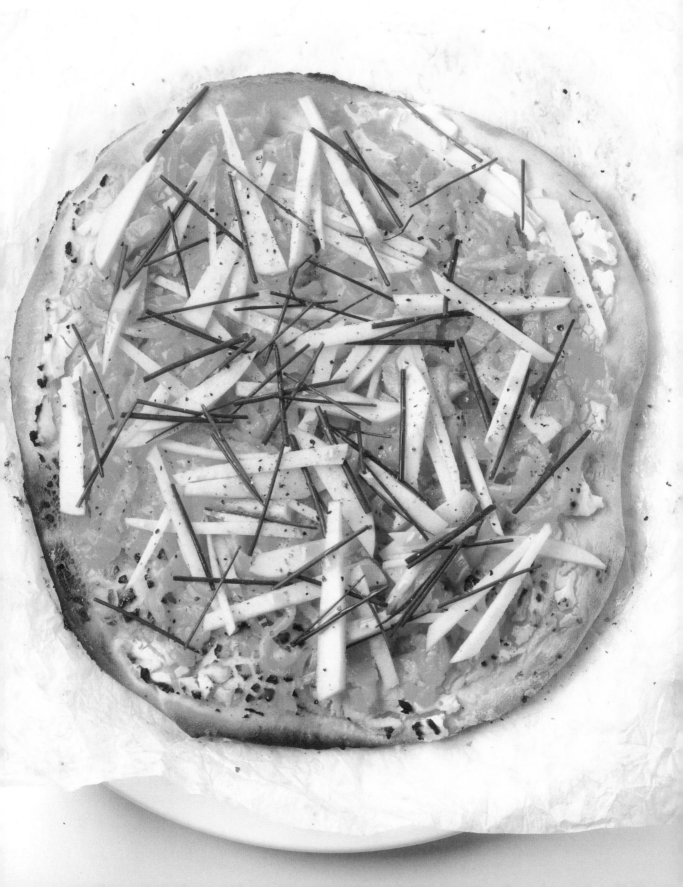

BACON AND SAGE TARTS

Pizza dough
2 balls (frozen)

Cream
4 tablespoons

Bacon
7 thin slices

Sage
2 sprigs

Olive oil
4 tablespoons

 **Salt, pepper**

**Preparation:
15 minutes
Cooking:
25 minutes**

• Preheat the oven to 220°C. Stretch out the **pizza dough** on a large baking sheet.

• Top with **cream**, **bacon slices** and **sage leaves**. Bake in the oven for 25 minutes.

• Remove from the oven, drizzle with **olive oil**, season with salt and pepper and serve.

COLD RATATOUILLE WITH MINT

Sweet onion
x 1

Peppers, mixed
x 2

Courgettes
x 2

Aubergine
x 1 (small)

Olive oil
6 tablespoons

Mint
20 leaves

 Salt, pepper

**Preparation:
25 minutes
Cooking:
45 minutes**

• Chop the **onion**. Cut the **peppers**, **courgettes** and **aubergine** into small cubes.

• Heat the **olive oil** and sear the vegetables without browning. Season with salt and pepper and cook for 45 minutes over low heat, without browning.

• Leave to cool, add the chopped **mint** and serve.

VEGETABLE TIAN

Potatoes
x 2 (large)

Aubergine
x 1

Courgettes
x 2

Tomatoes
x 3

Dried thyme
1 tablespoon

Olive oil
6 tablespoons

 Salt, pepper

**Preparation:
15 minutes
Cooking:
45 minutes**

• Preheat the oven to 180°C. Wash all the vegetables and cut into thin strips.
• Arrange in layers in a gratin dish and season with salt, pepper, dried **thyme** and **olive oil**.
• Bake in the oven for 45 minutes and serve in the gratin dish.

AUBERGINE GRATIN

Aubergines
x 2

Mozzarella
2 balls (250 g)

Chopped tomatoes
300 g

Parmesan
100 g

Olive oil
2 tablespoons

 **Salt, pepper**

**Preparation:
25 minutes
Cooking:
1 hour**

• Preheat the oven to 180°C. Wash the **aubergines** and cut into slices lengthways. Cut the **mozzarella** in rounds.
• Fill a gratin dish with alternate layers of **tomatoes**, **mozzarella** and **aubergines**, season with salt and pepper, sprinkle with grated **Parmesan** and drizzle with **olive oil**.
• Bake in the oven for 1 hour and serve with a salad.

SWISS CHARD AND CHEESE GRATIN

Swiss chard
1 kg

Cream
600 ml

Grated cheese
200 g

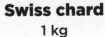 **Salt, pepper**

**Preparation:
15 minutes
Cooking:
30 minutes**

• Preheat the oven to 180°C. Wash the **chard**, cut into pieces and place in boiling salted water for 5 minutes. Drain, leave to cool and mix with the **cream** and **cheese**.
• Season the mixture with salt and pepper, transfer to a gratin dish and bake for 30 minutes.
• When the crust is nicely browned, serve in the gratin dish with a salad.

COURGETTE FRITTERS IN A SALAD

Rocket
2 handfuls (80 g)

Courgettes
x 2

Eggs
x 2 (separated)

Flour
100 g

Beer
100 ml

Mint
10 leaves

 **Salt, pepper
+ oil for frying**

**Preparation:
15 minutes
Cooking:
5 minutes**

• Wash the **rocket**. Cut the **courgettes** into rounds.
• Beat the **egg whites** until stiff. Mix together the **flour, beer** and **egg yolks**.
• Add the **egg whites** to the mixture. Heat the **oil**.
• Dip the **courgettes** in the batter and deep fry. Serve the fritters hot with the **rocket** and chopped **mint**.

COURGETTE GRATIN

Courgettes
650 g

Grated cheese
200 g

  Salt, pepper

Preparation:
5 minutes
Cooking:
30 minutes

• Preheat the oven to 180°C. Wash the **courgettes** and grate in a food processor.
• Mix in a gratin dish with the **grated cheese**, season with salt and pepper and bake for 30 minutes.

HONEY-GLAZED TURNIPS

Baby turnips
2 bunches

Liquid honey
12 tablespoons

  Salt, pepper

**Preparation:
15 minutes
Cooking:
40 minutes**

• Trim and peel the **turnips**. Cook for 30 minutes in a saucepan of boiling salted water (they should melt in the mouth).

• Heat the **honey** in a large frying pan, add the **turnips** and caramelise over a high heat for 6 to 8 minutes, stirring regularly.

• Season with salt and pepper and serve as an accompaniment to duck.

POTATO WEDGES WITH SALT AND ROSEMARY

Potatoes
1 kg (waxy)

Olive oil
6 tablespoons

Rosemary
2 sprigs

Sea salt
1.5 tablespoons

 Pepper

Preparation:
10 minutes
Cooking:
30 minutes

• Preheat the oven to 180°C. Wash the **potatoes** and cut into wedges.

• Arrange on a baking sheet, drizzle with **olive oil** and bake in the oven for 30 minutes, turning occasionally so they brown on all sides.

• Chop the **rosemary**, mix with the **sea salt**, season the wedges and eat with ketchup.

SWEET POTATO CHIPS

Avocados
x 2

Lemons
x 2

Sweet potatoes
1 kg

Sea salt
4 teaspoons

Curry powder
4 teaspoons

 **Salt, pepper**

**Preparation:
15 minutes
Cooking:
25 minutes**

• Peel the **avocados**, remove the stones and mix the flesh with the juice of the **lemons**, season with salt and pepper and refrigerate.

• Peel the **sweet potatoes** and cut in even-sized batons. Fry in a deep-fat fryer until golden brown and then drain. Season with **sea salt** and **curry powder** and mix well. Serve with the avocado sauce.

GRATIN DAUPHINOIS

Garlic
2 cloves

Potatoes
1 kg

Cream
400 ml

Grated nutmeg
½ teaspoon

 **Salt, pepper**

👤👤👤👤

🕐

**Preparation:
15 minutes
Cooking:
1 hour**

• Preheat the oven to 170°C. Peel the **garlic cloves** and slice thinly. Peel the **potatoes** and cut into thin slices.
• Arrange layers of **potatoes**, **garlic** and **cream** in a gratin dish, season between the layers with salt, pepper and **nutmeg**, and finish with a layer of **cream**.
• Bake in the oven for 1 hour. Serve very hot.

GOUDA AND CUMIN SEED TARTIFLETTE

Sweet onion
x 1

Potatoes
x 4 (large)

Lardons
200 g

Cumin-seed Gouda
400 g

Cumin
1 teaspoon

 **Salt, pepper**

**Preparation:
10 minutes
Cooking:
30 minutes**

• Preheat the oven to 170°C. Peel the **onion** and slice thinly. Peel and slice the **potatoes**.

• Arrange the **potatoes**, **lardons** and **onion** in a gratin dish.

• Top with **Gouda** and **cumin**, bake in the oven for 30 minutes and serve.

PEPPERS FILLED WITH RICOTTA AND OLIVES

Ricotta
2 pots (each 250 g)

Dried thyme
1 teaspoon

Tapenade
2 tablespoons

Green peppers
x 2 (large)

Tomato purée
500 ml

 **Salt, pepper**

**Preparation:
10 minutes
Cooking:
40 minutes**

- Preheat the oven to 180°C. Mix together the **ricotta, thyme** and **tapenade**.
- Cut the **peppers** in two, scoop out the contents and fill with the **ricotta** and **tapenade** mixture.
- In an oven dish beat the **tomato purée** with 250 ml water. Arrange the **peppers** on top, season with salt and pepper and bake in the oven for 40 minutes. Eat hot or cold.

BAKED PEPPERS WITH PARSLEY

Peppers, mixed
x 8

Flat-leaf parsley
8 sprigs

Garlic
6 cloves

Olive oil
6 tablespoons

 **Salt, pepper**

👤👤👤👤

🕐

**Preparation:
20 minutes
Cooking:
35 minutes**

• Preheat the oven to 180°C. Bake the **peppers** for 35 minutes. Wash and chop the **parsley**. Peel and press the **garlic**.

• Remove the **peppers** from the oven, remove the skins and seeds and chop the flesh. Pour the cooking juices into a large bowl, add the **peppers**, **oil**, **garlic** and **parsley**, season with salt and pepper and mix well.

PUMPKIN GRATIN WITH CHEESE

Fourme d'Ambert cheese
200 g

Pumpkin
800 g

Cream
2 tablespoons

Walnut oil
1 tablespoon

 Salt, pepper

👤👤👤👤

🕐

Preparation:
10 minutes
Cooking:
45 minutes

• Preheat the oven to 170°C. Cut the **cheese** into pieces.
• Peel and slice the **pumpkin**.
• Fill a gratin dish with alternate layers of **pumpkin** and **cheese**.
• Add the **cream** and **walnut oil**, season with salt and pepper and bake in the oven for 45 minutes.
• Serve very hot.

MOZZARELLA AND FIG SKEWERS

Rocket
2 two handfuls (80 g)

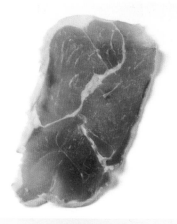

Air-dried ham
4 slices

Mozzarella
1 ball (125 g)

Figs
x 4

Olive oil
4 tablespoons

 **Salt, pepper**

**Preparation:
10 minutes
Cooking:
5 minutes**

• Preheat the oven to 180°C. Wash the **rocket**. Cut the **ham** slices into four, the **mozzarella** into eight and the figs into three.

• Arrange the three ingredients alternately on four skewers. Place in an oven dish and bake for 5 minutes.

• Arrange on a serving dish with the **rocket**, drizzle with **olive oil** and season with salt and pepper.

BAKED TOMATOES FILLED WITH EGGS

Tomatoes
x 4 (large)

Olive oil
4 tablespoons

Eggs
x 4

Balsamic vinegar
2 tablespoons

 Salt, pepper

**Preparation:
5 minutes
Cooking:
15 minutes**

• Preheat the oven to 170°C. Cut lids off the **tomatoes** and scoop out the contents.
• Place in a large oven dish, drizzle with **olive oil** and bake in the oven for 5 minutes.
• Break an **egg** into each **tomato**, season with salt and pepper and bake for a further 10 minutes.
• Drizzle with a dash of **vinegar** and serve.

LEEK GRATIN WITH REBLOCHON CHEESE

Leeks
400 g

Reblochon cheese
250 g

 Salt, pepper

👥👥👥👥

🕐

Preparation:
10 minutes
Cooking:
30 minutes

• Preheat the oven to 180°C. Cut the **leeks** in half lengthways, wash in plenty of water, dry and arrange in an oven dish.

• Cut the **Reblochon** in slices, arrange on top of the **leeks** and bake in the oven for 30 minutes.

• When the top is nicely browned, remove from the oven and serve with a salad.

PEAR GRATIN WITH PARMESAN

Pears
x 4

Parmesan
100 g

Salt, pepper

👤👤👤👤

**Preparation:
5 minutes
Cooking:
30 minutes**

• Preheat the oven to 180°C. Peel the **pears** and cut in quarters. Roughly chop the **Parmesan**.
• Arrange the **pears** in an oven dish, top with **Parmesan**, salt lightly, pepper and bake for 30 minutes.
• Eat as a main dish with a salad or as an accompaniment to poultry or roast veal.

NAVARIN OF LAMB WITH VEGETABLES

Diced stewing lamb
1.2 kg (shoulder or leg)

Olive oil
4 tablespoons

Thyme
2 sprigs

Chopped tomatoes
2 tins (800 g)

Garden peas
200 g (fresh or frozen)

Mange-tout peas
200 g

 Salt, pepper

**Preparation:
5 minutes
Cooking:
1 hour 25 minutes**

• Sear the **lamb** in the **olive oil** in a casserole.
• Add the **thyme** and the **tomatoes**, season with salt and pepper, reduce the heat, cover and simmer for 1 hour over low heat. Add the **garden** and **mange-tout peas** and cook for a further 20 minutes before serving.

160

LAMB WITH POTATOES

Potatoes
x 2 (large)

Sweet onions
x 2

Tomatoes
x 3

Lamb breasts
x 2 (600 g)

Thyme
2 teaspoons

White wine
1 glass (150 ml)

 **Salt, pepper**

**Preparation:
10 minutes
Cooking:
2 hours**

• Preheat the oven to 170°C. Peel the **potatoes** and **onions** and cut in thin slices. Cut the **tomatoes** in rings and the **lamb breasts** in four.

• Mix all the ingredients together in a large oven dish, season with salt and pepper, add the **white wine** and 300 ml water and cook in the oven for 2 hours. Serve in the oven dish accompanied by a salad.

LAMB SKEWERS WITH MANGO

Mint
30 leaves (small)

Mangoes
x 2

Lamb
800 g

Olive oil
4 tablespoons

Balsamic vinegar
4 tablespoons

 **Salt, pepper**

**Preparation:
10 minutes
Cooking:
20 minutes**

• Preheat the oven to 180°C. Wash the **mint**. Peel the **mangoes** and cut the **mangoes** and **lamb** into small pieces. Arrange the **lamb** and **mango** alternately on four skewers.
• Brown the skewers for 20 minutes under the oven grill.
• Arrange on a serving dish, drizzle with **olive oil** and **vinegar**, sprinkle with **mint**, season with salt and pepper and enjoy.

SLOW-ROASTED SHOULDER OF LAMB

Shoulder of lamb
x 1 (with bone)

Flat-leaf parsley
6 sprigs

Coriander
1 bunch

Garlic
6 cloves

Green chilli
x 1 (small)

Olive oil
150 ml

 Salt, pepper

Preparation:
15 minutes
Cooking:
2 hours

• Preheat the oven to 160°C. Place the **lamb** in a large roasting dish, season with salt and pepper and cook for 2 hours, basting occasionally.

• Wash the **parsley** and **coriander** and pick off the leaves.

• Peel and chop the **garlic cloves**, remove the seeds from the **chilli**, chop and mix both with the **olive oil** and the **herbs** to make a sauce. Serve the shoulder of **lamb** with the sauce, accompanied by a rocket salad and thyme for decoration, if desired.

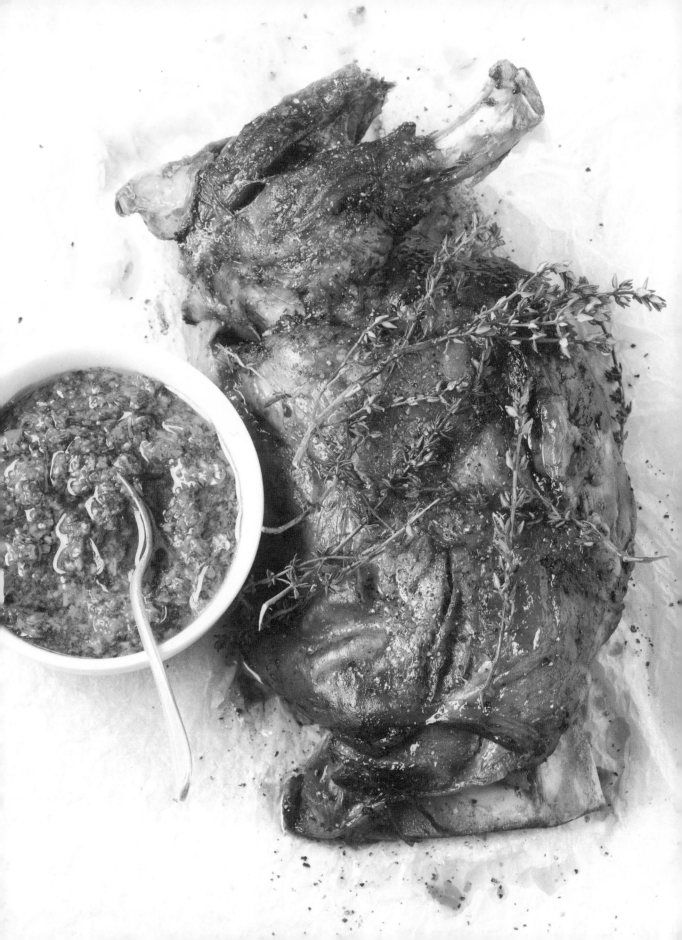

7-HOUR LEG OF LAMB

Leg of lamb
x 1

Garlic
10 cloves

Sweet wine
½ bottle (375 ml)

Stock
500 ml

Rosemary
2 sprigs

Ruby port
½ bottle (37.5 cl)

 **Salt, pepper**

👤👤👤👤👤👤

🕐
**Preparation:
10 minutes
Cooking:
7 hours**

• Preheat the oven to 160°C. Place the leg of **lamb** in a large cast-iron casserole, add the crushed **garlic**, **wine**, **port**, **stock** and **rosemary**.
• Cover and cook in the oven for 7 hours, basting occasionally. Add a little water if the sauce reduces too much. Season with salt and pepper. Serve the **lamb** accompanied by couscous.

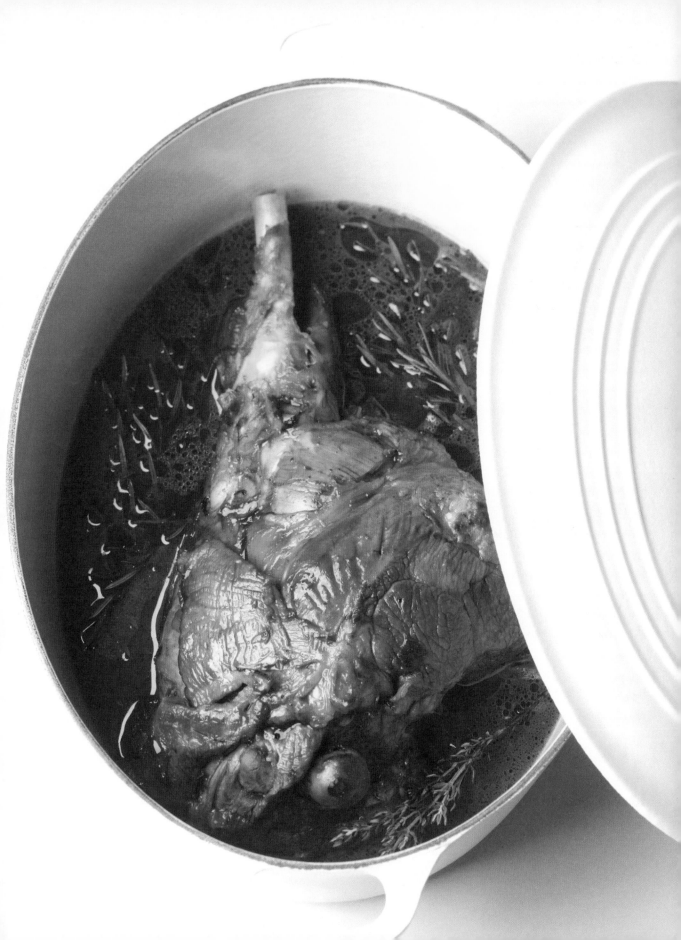

BLANQUETTE OF VEAL WITH ASPARAGUS

Veal shoulder
1.2 kg (diced)

Water or stock
500 ml

Green asparagus
x 4 stems (large)

Button mushrooms
200 g

Double cream
330 ml

Flour
2 tablespoons

 **Salt, pepper**

**Preparation:
15 minutes
Cooking:
1 hour 15 minutes**

• Stew the **veal** in the **stock** for 1 hour over low heat. Peel the **asparagus** and cut into pieces and slice the **mushrooms** thinly. Remove the meat from the pan. Mix the **cream** with the **flour** and beat into the **stock**.

• Add the **asparagus** and **mushrooms** and simmer for a further 10 minutes, stirring continuously. Return the meat to the sauce and season with salt and pepper.

KIDNEYS WITH MUSTARD SAUCE

Veal kidneys
x 4

Wholegrain mustard
4 tablespoons

Dijon mustard
1 tablespoon

Bouquet garni
x 1

Cream
600 ml

 Salt, pepper

👥👥👥👥

🕐

Preparation:
5 minutes
Cooking:
10 minutes

• Cut the **kidneys** into bite-sized pieces and brown lightly in a frying pan with 2 tablespoons of oil.
• Cook for 5 minutes, then stir in the **wholegrain mustard**, **Dijon mustard**, **herbs** and **cream**.
• Season with salt and pepper, cook for a further 5 minutes and serve with fresh pasta.

VEAL CHOPS WITH MORELS

Dried morels
50 g

Double cream
330 ml

Veal chops
x 2 (450 g each)

Soy sauce
4 tablespoons

  Salt, pepper

**Preparation:
35 minutes
Cooking: 25 minutes
Soaking: 30 minutes**

• Soak the **morels** in 500 ml water for 30 minutes. Remove the **morels**, strain the water and reduce to three-quarters in a saucepan. Beat in the **cream** and reduce for 10 minutes over high heat.

• Sear the **veal chops** and fry for 5 minutes on each side in a sauteuse pan.

• Deglaze with the **soy sauce**, add the **morels** and the **cream**, cook for 5 minutes and serve.

VEAL ROLLS WITH ASPARAGUS

Green asparagus
x 16 stems

Veal escalopes
x 4

Pesto
2 tablespoons

Olive oil
2 tablespoons

 **Salt, pepper**

**Preparation:
10 minutes
Cooking:
25 minutes**

• Preheat the oven to 180°C. Peel and trim the **asparagus** and blanch for 3 minutes.

• Brush the **escalopes** with **pesto**, place four **asparagus** stems in the middle of each, season with salt and pepper, roll up and tie with string.

• Season again with salt and pepper, drizzle with **olive oil** and bake in the oven for 25 minutes. Cut into thick slices and serve.

VEAL ESCALOPES WITH CHORIZO

Veal escalopes
x 4

Chorizo
4 slices (large)

Thyme
8 sprigs

Sage
4 leaves

  Salt, pepper

**Preparation:
10 minutes
Cooking:
25 minutes**

• Preheat the oven to 180°C. Cut the **escalopes** in two and place a slice of **chorizo** on each piece (you can fix them in place with cocktail sticks).
• Add the **thyme** and **sage**, season with salt and pepper and bake in the oven for 25 minutes. Serve in the oven dish with a rocket salad or fresh pasta.

OSSO BUCO WITH TOMATOES AND ORANGES

Oranges
x 4

Olive oil
4 tablespoons

Veal shank portions
x 8

Rosemary
2 sprigs

Chopped tomatoes
2 tins (800 g)

 **Salt, pepper**

👤👤👤👤

🕐

**Preparation:
15 minutes
Cooking:
1 hour 30 minutes**

• Grate the peel of the **oranges** and squeeze out the juice. Heat the **oil** in a casserole dish, brown the **veal** on both sides, add the **orange juice** and **peel**, the **rosemary** and the **chopped tomatoes**.

• Season with salt and pepper and simmer for 1 hour 30 minutes over a very low heat. Serve in the casserole dish, accompanied by fresh pasta.

POT-ROAST VEAL WITH ASPARAGUS

Green asparagus
x 20 stems

Tarragon
1 bunch

Olive oil
4 tablespoons

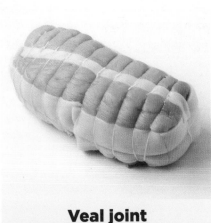

Veal joint
(900 g to 1 kg)

Garlic
4 cloves

 **Salt, pepper**

**Preparation:
15 minutes
Cooking:
40 minutes**

• Peel the **asparagus**. Wash the **tarragon**, remove the leaves and chop roughly.

• Heat the **olive oil** in a casserole, lightly brown the **veal** with the chopped **garlic**, season with salt and pepper, cover and cook for 25 minutes.

• Add 1 glass of water and the **asparagus**, cook for a further 10 minutes, then add the **tarragon**. Mix together and serve the meat in slices.

STEWED VEAL WITH OLIVES

Olive oil
4 tablespoons

Stewing veal
1 kg (diced)

Dry white wine
½ bottle (37.5 cl)

Bouquet garni
x 1

Tomato purée
500 ml

Green and black olives
200 g (stoned)

 **Salt, pepper**

🕐

**Preparation:
15 minutes
Cooking:
2 hours**

• Heat the **oil** in a casserole dish. Lightly brown the **veal**, add the **white wine**, **herbs**, **tomato purée** and **olives**.
• Simmer for 2 hours over a low heat, stirring occasionally.
• Add a little water if the sauce reduces too much. Serve with fresh pasta.

BAVETTE STEAKS WITH CRISPY SHALLOTS

Shallots
x 4 (long)

Milk
20 ml

Flour
1 tablespoon

Flat-leaf parsley
8 sprigs

Bavette steaks
x 4 (180 g each)

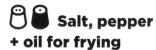 **Salt, pepper
+ oil for frying**

**Preparation:
15 minutes
Cooking:
15 minutes**

• Peel the **shallots** and slice thinly. Heat the **oil** in a saucepan.

• Dip the **shallots** in **milk** and **flour** and fry until golden. Wash and chop the **parsley**.

• Sear the **steaks** in 1 tablespoon oil for 2 minutes on each side. Season with salt and pepper. Arrange on a serving dish, top with the **shallots** and **parsley** and serve with a salad.

BEEF BOURGUIGNON

Stewing beef
1.2 kg (diced)

Sweet onion
x 1 (large)

Flour
1 tablespoon

Red wine
1 bottle (75 cl)

Lardons
200 g

Button mushrooms
250 g

 **Salt, pepper**

👤👤👤👤

**Preparation:
10 minutes
Cooking:
2 hours 35 minutes**

• Slice the **onion** thinly. Heat the oil in a cast-iron casserole. Lightly brown the **beef** on all sides and add the **onion** and **flour**.

• Cook for 5 minutes, then add the **red wine** and 300 ml water. Cover and simmer for 2 hours over very low heat. Wash and chop the **mushrooms** and add to the pan with the **lardons**. Cook for a further 30 minutes and season with salt and pepper, and thyme if you wish.

BEEF WITH CARROTS

Carrots
1 kg

Sweet onions
x 2

Olive oil
3 tablespoons

Brisket of beef
1.2 kg

Thyme
4 sprigs

Bay leaves
x 3

 **Salt, pepper**

**Preparation:
10 minutes
Cooking:
2 hours**

• Peel the **carrots** and cut into thick rounds. Peel the **onions** and slice thinly.

• Heat the **oil** in a casserole dish to smoking point, lightly brown the **beef** and add the **onions**, **carrots**, **thyme** and **bay leaves**.

• Season with salt and pepper, cover with water, add the lid and simmer for 2 hours over very low heat.

SAVOURY MEAT BALLS

Basil
20 leaves

Sweet onion
x 1

Minced beef
700 g

Ketchup
4 tablespoons

Olive oil
4 tablespoons

Gazpacho
300 ml

 **Salt, pepper**

👤👤👤👤

🕐

**Preparation:
20 minutes
Cooking:
5 minutes**

• Preheat the oven to 180°C. Wash and chop the **basil**. Peel the **onion** and slice thinly. Mix all the ingredients except the **gazpacho** together in a large bowl.
• Season with salt and pepper and form into 12 balls. Bake in the oven for 5 minutes (they should not cook very much). Pour the cold **gazpacho** into 4 deep plates. Add the warm meatballs and serve.

COLOURFUL BEEF CHEEK STEW

Beef cheeks
x 2

Thyme
4 sprigs

Golden Ball turnips
x 6

White beetroot
x 4 (small)

Sweet potato
x 1

Salt, pepper

**Preparation:
10 minutes
Cooking:
2 hours 50 minutes**

• Peel and chop the vegetables. Place the **beef cheeks, thyme, turnips** and **beetroot** in a casserole dish, cover with water and cook for 2 hours 30 minutes over a very low heat, skimming regularly.

• Add the chopped **sweet potato** and cook for a further 20 minutes. Season with salt and pepper and serve.

CHILLI CON CARNE

Red onions
x 2

Minced beef
600 g

Paprika
2 tablespoons

Red kidney beans
2 tins (400 g each)

Tomato purée
500 ml

 **Salt, pepper**

**Preparation:
15 minutes
Cooking:
50 minutes**

• Peel and chop the **onions**. Sear the **beef** and **onions** in 2 tablespoons of oil, add the **paprika**, brown for 5 minutes, then add the drained **beans** and the **tomato purée**.

• Cook for 45 minutes over a low heat, stirring regularly.

• Season with salt and pepper and serve with pieces of fresh avocado.

ROAST RIB OF BEEF WITH FALSE BÉARNAISE

Mayonnaise
200 g

Tarragon mustard
1 tablespoon

Vinegar
1 teaspoon

Tarragon
1 bunch

Thick rib of beef
x 1 (1 kg)

 **Salt, pepper**

**Preparation:
15 minutes
Cooking:
12 minutes**

• Mix the **mayonnaise** with the **mustard**, **vinegar** and chopped **tarragon** to form a sauce. Preheat the oven to 180°C.

• Heat the oil in a frying pan, brown the **beef** for 1 minute on each side, season with salt and pepper and roast for 10 minutes, turning once.

• Leave to rest for 5 minutes under a sheet of foil and serve with the sauce.

BEEF STEW

Basil
1 bunch

Dried tomatoes
x 10

Olive oil
4 tablespoons

Stewing beef
1.2 kg (chopped)

Garlic
4 cloves

Red wine
1 bottle (75 cl)

 **Salt, pepper**

👤👤👤👤👤👤

🕐

**Preparation:
25 minutes
Cooking:
2 hours**

• Wash the **basil** and pick off the leaves. Cut the dried **tomatoes** into pieces. Heat the **oil** in a casserole. Brown the **beef** on all sides.

• Crush the **garlic** with the skin on and add to the pan with the **red wine**. Simmer for 2 hours over very low heat. Season with salt and pepper, add the **basil** and **dried tomatoes**, mix well and serve with fresh pasta.

FRESH BEEF TARTARE

Sweet onion
x 1

Basil
1 bunch

Coriander
1 bunch

Olive oil
4 tablespoons

Ketchup
4 tablespoons

Minced beef
700 g

 **Salt, pepper**

👥👥👥👥

🕐

**Preparation:
10 minutes**

• Peel and chop the **onion**, wash, pick off the **basil** and **coriander** leaves and chop with the stems.

• Mix all the above with the **oil**, **ketchup** and **beef**.

• Season with salt and pepper and serve.

BEEF STIR-FRY WITH THAI BASIL

Beef topside
600 g

Thai basil
40 leaves

Garlic
4 cloves

Olive oil
6 tablespoons

Soy sauce
4 tablespoons

  **Salt, pepper**

👫👫

🕐

**Preparation:
10 minutes
Cooking:
5 minutes**

• Cut the **beef** into small pieces, wash the **basil** and peel and chop the **garlic**.

• In a frying pan, sear the **beef** and **garlic** for 3 minutes with the **olive oil**.

• Turn off the heat, add the **soy sauce** and **basil**, mix together and season with salt and pepper.

PAVÉ RUMP STEAK WITH ROQUEFORT

Pavé rump steaks
x 4

Roquefort cheese
200 g

Preparation:
5 minutes
Cooking:
10 minutes

• Cut the **Roquefort** into small pieces.
• Sear the **steaks** in a hot dry pan and cook for 3 minutes on each side.
• Remove from the heat and leave to rest for 3 minutes, cover with **Roquefort**, mix and serve.

PORK KNUCKLE IN HAY

Salted pork knuckle
x 2 (cooked, with bones)

Hay
100 g

 **Salt, pepper**

• Place the **hay** and **pork knuckles** in a casserole dish, cover with water and a lid and cook for 45 minutes over a low heat. Leave the **pork** to cool in the stock.
• Remove the meat, rinse, cut into pieces and serve with mashed potato.

Preparation:
5 minutes
Cooking:
45 minutes

PORK RIBS WITH BBQ SAUCE

Pork ribs
1.2 kg

Ketchup
4 tablespoons

Soy sauce
4 tablespoons

Liquid honey
2 tablespoons

Thyme
4 sprigs

Salt, pepper

**Preparation:
10 minutes
Cooking:
50 minutes**

• Preheat the oven to 170°C. Cut the **ribs** into large chunks and cook in the oven for 30 minutes.
• Remove from the oven, remove the fat and return the **ribs** to the roasting pan.
• Cover with a mixture of **ketchup**, **soy sauce**, **honey** and **thyme**, then return the **ribs** to the oven for 20 minutes, basting regularly to coat them well. Season with salt and pepper and serve.

PORK FILET MIGNON WITH CHEESE

Pork filets mignons
x 2

Mimolette cheese
300 g (sliced)

 **Salt, pepper**

👪👪👪👪

🕐

**Preparation:
10 minutes
Cooking:
45 minutes**

• Preheat the oven to 180°C. Sear the **filets mignons** in a frying pan with 2 tablespoons of oil. Place in an oven dish and make slits all the way along the meat. Cut the **Mimolette** slices in four, fold in half and insert in the slits in the meat.

• Season with salt and pepper and roast for 45 minutes. Add ½ glass of water halfway through and allow a crust to form.

PORK WITH CHERRIES

Cherries
x 24

Pork ribs (back)
x 4

 **Salt, pepper**

Preparation:
15 minutes
Cooking:
35 minutes

• Cut the **pork** into cubes. Sear the meat in a frying pan with 1 tablespoon of oil.
• Brown for 25 minutes, stirring regularly, then add the **cherries**. Cook for a further 10 minutes, season with salt and pepper and serve.

CARAMELISED PORK

Pork shoulder
800 g

Liquid honey
6 tablespoons

Soy sauce
6 tablespoons

Sesame seeds
1 tablespoon

 **Salt, pepper**

👤👤👤👤

🕐

Preparation:
5 minutes
Cooking:
1 hour 30 minutes

• Preheat the oven to 170°C. Roast the whole **pork shoulder** for 1 hour.

• Remove the fat, then add the **honey** and **soy sauce**.

• Cook for a further 30 minutes, basting regularly with the sauce to coat well. Sprinkle with **sesame seeds**.

• Cut the meat into small pieces, cover with the **honey** and **soy sauce** caramel and serve with rice.

POT-ROASTED PORK WITH PEPPERS

Peppers, mixed
1 kg

Garlic
8 cloves

Olive oil
4 tablespoons

Roasting pork
1.2 kg

Thyme
4 sprigs

Balsamic vinegar
4 tablespoons

 **Salt, pepper**

👤👤👤👤👤👤

🕐

**Preparation:
8 minutes
Cooking:
45 minutes**

• Remove the stems and seeds from the **peppers** and slice thinly. Crush the **garlic cloves** with the skins on.

• Heat the **oil** in a casserole dish, sear the **pork**, add the **peppers**, **garlic** and **thyme**, season with salt and pepper, cover and cook for 45 minutes.

• Add the **vinegar**, mix in and serve.

STUFFED CABBAGE

Savoy cabbage
8 leaves

Sausage meat
200 g

Minced veal
200 g

Raisins
50 g

Egg
x 1

Olive oil
2 tablespoons

 **Salt, pepper**

**Preparation:
20 minutes
Cooking:
40 minutes**

• Preheat the oven to 170°C. Place the **cabbage** leaves in boiling water for 2 minutes, rinse in cold water, remove the hard stems and cut the leaves in two.
• Mix the **sausage meat** with the **minced veal**, **raisins** and **egg**, and season with salt and pepper.
• Spread out the **cabbage**, arrange the stuffing on the leaves, roll up one at a time and place in an oven dish. Drizzle with **olive oil** and bake in the oven for 35 minutes.

CHICORY WITH COUNTRY HAM

Pouring cream
250 ml

Grated cheese
250 g

Air-dried ham
4 thin slices

Chicory
x 4

 Pepper

**Preparation:
10 minutes
Cooking:
25 minutes**

• Preheat the oven to 180°C. Mix the **cream** with the **cheese**. Cut the slices of **ham** in two lengthways.
• Cut the **chicory** heads in two and wrap each in a half-slice of **ham**.
• Arrange in an oven dish, cover with the **cream** and **cheese**, season with pepper and bake in the oven for 25 minutes until the crust has browned.

ORIENTAL MEAT BALLS

Minced beef
200 g

Sausage meat
200 g

Cumin seeds
2 tablespoons

Egg
x 1

Peppers, mixed
x 3

Olive oil
2 tablespoons

**Preparation:
10 minutes
Cooking:
35 minutes**

• Preheat the oven to 170°C. Mix together the **mince**, **sausage meat**, **cumin** and **egg**. Knead and form into even-sized balls.

• Cut the **peppers** into strips. Arrange all these in an oven dish, drizzle with **olive oil**, season with salt and pepper and bake in the oven for 35 minutes.

• Add 2 tablespoons of water, mix in, and serve.

PORK KNUCKLE WITH CABBAGE AND BEER

Red cabbage
x 1

Butter
80 g

Salted pork knuckle
x 4 (cooked, bone in)

Cumin
2 tablespoons

Beer
660 ml

Prunes
x 8

 Pepper

**Preparation:
15 minutes
Cooking:
2 hours**

• Grate the **red cabbage** in a food processor. Melt the **butter** in a casserole dish, sear the **pork knuckles** and brown lightly.

• Add the **red cabbage**, 200 ml water and the **cumin**, cover and simmer over a low heat for 1 hour, stirring regularly.

• Add the **beer** and **prunes** and simmer for a further 1 hour so the **pork** melts in the mouth. Season with pepper.

MERGUEZ SAUSAGES WITH TOMATOES

Rosemary
2 sprigs

Cherry tomatoes
500 g (mixed colours)

Merguez sausages
x 4

 **Salt, pepper**

**Preparation:
10 minutes
Cooking:
20 minutes**

• Preheat the oven to 170°C. Chop the **rosemary**.
• Cut the **tomatoes** in two. Prick the **sausages** with a fork and place in an oven dish.
• Bake in the oven for 10 minutes, then add the **tomatoes** and cook for a further 10 minutes. Sprinkle with **rosemary**, season with salt and pepper, mix well and serve with mashed potato.

POTATO AND BLACK PUDDING BAKE

Potatoes
400 g

Black pudding
600 g

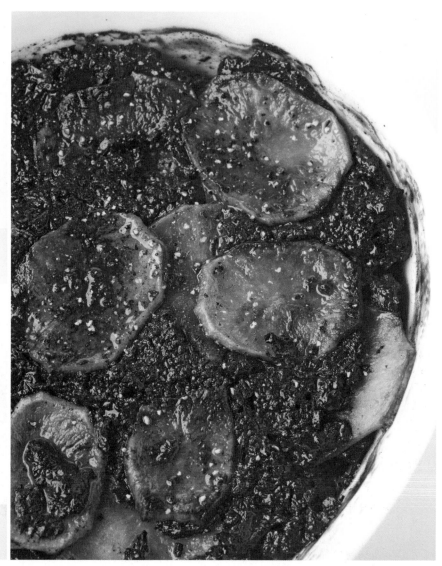

 **Salt, pepper**

👨👨👨👨

🕐

**Preparation:
10 minutes
Cooking:
45 minutes**

• Preheat the oven to 180°C. Peel the **potatoes** and cut in thin slices.
• Remove the skin from the **black pudding**. Mix the contents with the sliced **potatoes** in an oven dish.
• Season with salt and pepper, press down firmly and bake in the oven for 45 minutes.

CHICKEN DRUMSTICKS WITH GINGERBREAD

Gingerbread
4 slices

Chicken drumsticks
x 8

  **Salt, pepper**

👤👤👤👤

🕐

**Preparation:
10 minutes
Cooking:
45 minutes**

• Preheat the oven to 180°C. Mix the **gingerbread** with 80 ml water.
• Arrange the **chicken drumsticks** in a large oven dish, add the **gingerbread** and stir to ensure the drumsticks are well covered. Season with salt and pepper and bake in the oven for 45 minutes. Stir occasionally so they brown well. Eat with mustard or BBQ sauce.

CHICKEN LEGS WITH SAGE BUTTER

Chicken legs
x 4

Sage
1 bunch

Butter
100 g

 **Salt, pepper**

**Preparation:
10 minutes
Cooking:
45 minutes**

• Preheat the oven to 180°C. Cook the **chicken legs** for 40 minutes, basting regularly with the cooking juices, and season with salt and pepper.
• Wash the **sage** and pick off the leaves, cutting larger leaves in two.
• Heat the **butter** with the **sage** until it begins to brown. Pour the **sage** butter over the **chicken**. Leave to draw for 5 minutes, stirring occasionally.

CHICKEN WITH CASHEW NUTS

Chicken breasts
x 4

Sweet onion
x 1

Cashew nuts
200 g

Liquid honey
2 tablespoons

Soy sauce
4 tablespoons

Coriander
1 bunch

Preparation:
5 minutes
Cooking:
12 minutes

• Heat 3 tablespoons of oil in a frying pan. Cut the **chicken breasts** into pieces and sear.
• Chop the **onion** and **cashew nuts**, add to the pan and fry for 5 minutes, then add the **honey** and **soy sauce**.
• Stir-fry for a further 5 minutes and add the chopped **coriander** before serving.

CHICKEN WITH COCONUT AND LEMONGRASS

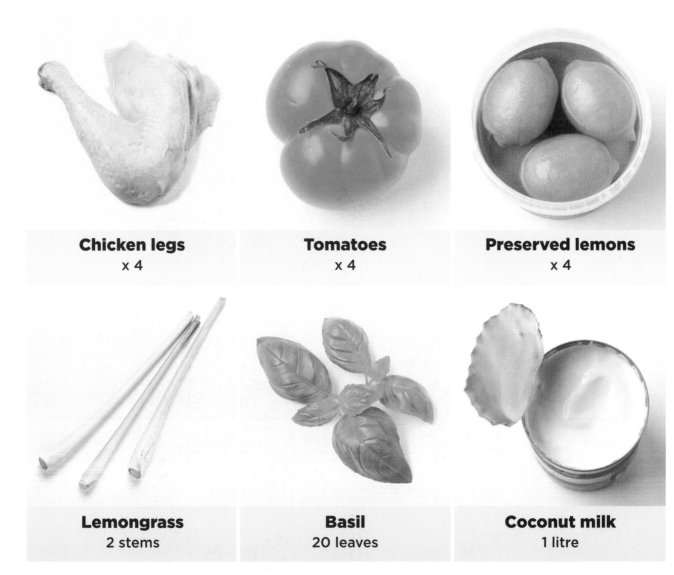

Chicken legs
x 4

Tomatoes
x 4

Preserved lemons
x 4

Lemongrass
2 stems

Basil
20 leaves

Coconut milk
1 litre

 **Salt, pepper**

**Preparation:
15 minutes
Cooking:
1 hour**

• Preheat the oven to 170°C. Cut the **chicken legs** in two and place in a large oven dish. Chop the **lemons**, slice the **lemongrass** thinly and add to the pan with the **tomatoes**, **basil** and **coconut milk**.

• Season with salt and pepper and cook in the oven for 1 hour, basting occasionally. When the **chicken** is thoroughly cooked, serve in the oven dish, accompanied by rice.

FRIED CHICKEN WITH AVOCADO CREAM

Avocados
x 2

Basil
10 leaves

Lemons
x 2

Chicken breasts
x 4

Eggs
x 2

Breadcrumbs
250 g

 **Salt, pepper + oil for frying**

**Preparation:
15 minutes
Cooking:
5 minutes**

• Peel the **avocados**, blend the flesh with the **basil** and the juice of the **lemons** and season with salt and pepper.
• Cut the **chicken** into strips.
• Dip the **chicken** strips in beaten **egg**, then in the **breadcrumbs**, and deep fry for 5 minutes.
• Serve with the **avocado** cream.

ROAST CHICKEN WITH PAPRIKA

Free-range chicken
x 1

Paprika
1 tablespoon

Curry powder
2 teaspoons

Lemons
x 2

Olive oil
4 tablespoons

 **Salt, pepper**

👤👤👤👤

🕐
**Preparation:
5 minutes
Cooking:
40 minutes**

• Preheat the oven to 180°C. Season the **chicken** with salt and pepper and rub with the **paprika**, **curry powder** and **olive oil**. Squeeze the juice from the **lemons** and add to the oven dish.

• Cook in the oven for 40 minutes, basting regularly. When the **chicken** is done, transfer to a dish and serve with the cooking juices.

CHICKEN STEW WITH CHESTNUTS

Dried porcini mushrooms
10 g

Chicken breasts
x 4

Double cream
600 ml

Chestnuts
400 g (jar)

 Salt, pepper

**Preparation:
15 minutes
Cooking:
30 minutes**

• Soak the **mushrooms** in 150 ml water. Cut the **chicken breasts** in pieces and sear in a casserole dish with 3 tablespoons of oil. Squeeze the moisture out of the **mushrooms**, chop and add to the pan with the water they were soaked in.

• Reduce for 5 minutes then add the **cream** and **chestnuts**. Simmer for 25 minutes over low heat. Season with salt and pepper and serve.

CHICKEN WITH PARSLEY AND PARMESAN

Chicken legs
x 4

Olive oil
2 tablespoons

Flat-leaf parsley
1 bunch

Lemons
x 4

Grated Parmesan
4 tablespoons

 **Salt, pepper**

**Preparation:
8 minutes
Cooking:
45 minutes**

• Preheat the oven to 180°C. Cut the **chicken legs** in two and cook for 40 minutes. Season with salt and pepper and drizzle with **olive oil**.

• Wash and chop the **parsley**. Grate the peel of the **lemons**, squeeze out the juice and mix all these with the **Parmesan**. Top the **chicken** with this mixture and cook for a further 5 minutes. Stir and serve.

240

CHICKEN WITH TARRAGON

Tarragon
6 sprigs

Chicken breasts
x 4

Paprika
4 tablespoons

Cream
330 ml

 **Salt, pepper**

👤👤👤👤

🕐
**Preparation:
5 minutes
Cooking:
12 minutes**

• Wash the **tarragon** and pick off the leaves.
• Heat 2 tablespoons of oil in a large frying pan, cut up the **chicken breasts**, sear, then add the **paprika** and **cream**.
• Reduce the heat and cook for 10 minutes, stirring continuously. Add the **tarragon**, season with salt and pepper and stir before serving.

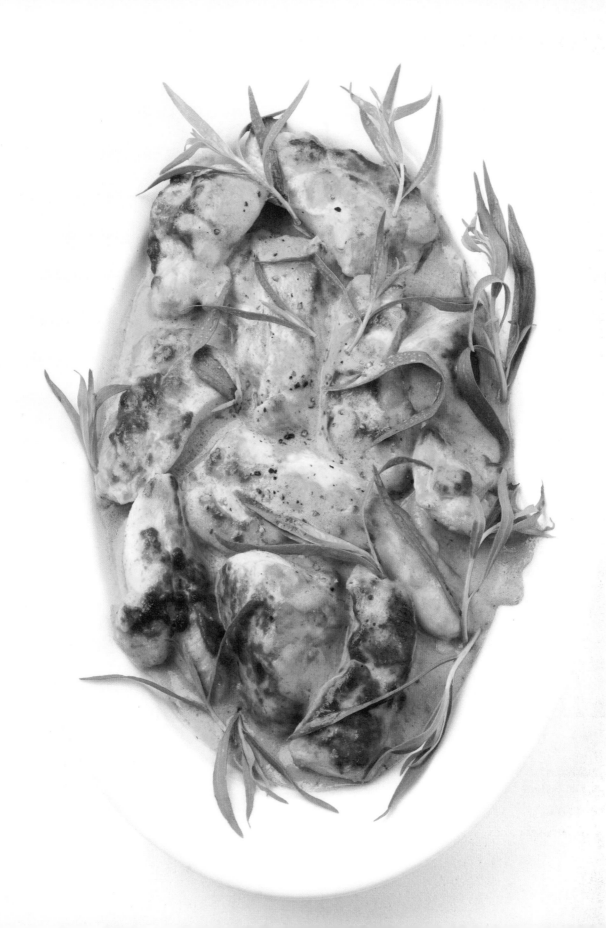

CURRIED COCONUT CHICKEN

Chicken legs
x 4

Onions
x 2 (large)

Coriander
1 bunch

Coconut milk
1 litre

Mild curry paste
4 tablespoons

 **Salt, pepper**

**Preparation:
15 minutes
Cooking:
45 minutes**

• Preheat the oven to 170°C. Cut the **chicken legs** in two and place in a large oven dish. Chop the **onion** and **coriander** and add to the **chicken** with the **coconut milk** and the **curry paste**.

• Season with salt and pepper and cook for 45 minutes, basting occasionally. Serve in the oven dish, accompanied by rice.

QUAILS WITH GRAPES

Air-dried ham
4 thin slices

Quails
x 4

Butter
80 g

Cognac
20 ml

Italian green grapes
40 (seedless)

Bouquet garni
x 1

 **Salt, pepper**

👤👤👤👤

🕐

**Preparation:
15 minutes
Cooking:
30 minutes**

• Wrap each **quail** in a slice of **ham** and tie with string. Sear in a casserole dish in the **butter**, add the **cognac**, flambé and cook for 20 minutes over low heat.
• Add the **grapes** and the **bouquet garni** and cook for a further 10 minutes, stirring regularly. Serve in the casserole dish, accompanied by a chestnut purée.

POTATOES WITH DUCK CONFIT

Potatoes
600 g (large)

Duck confit
4 legs

Tapenade
2 tablespoons

Thyme
4 sprigs

 **Salt, pepper**

👤👤👤👤

🕐
**Preparation:
10 minutes
Cooking:
45 minutes**

• Preheat the oven to 180°C. Peel the **potatoes** and cut into thin rounds. Debone and chop the **duck** and mix with the **tapenade** and the **thyme**.

• Fill a gratin dish with alternate layers of **duck** and **potatoes**. Bake in the oven for 45 minutes until the **potatoes** have browned. Serve with a salad.

DUCK BREASTS WITH PINEAPPLE

Coriander
10 sprigs

Duck breasts
x 2

Pineapple
6 slices (tinned

Soy sauce
4 tablespoons

**Preparation:
15 minutes
Cooking:
10 minutes**

• Wash the **coriander** and pick off the leaves. Remove the fat and cut the **duck breast** into small pieces.
• Cut each of the **pineapple** slices into six.
• Heat a large wok, lightly brown the **duck**, then add the **pineapple** and **soy sauce** and caramelise. Add the **coriander**, mix in and serve.

APRICOT AND ROSEMARY DUCK BREASTS

Duck breasts
x 2

Rosemary
4 sprigs

Apricots
x 12 (firm)

Liquid honey
2 tablespoons

Soy sauce
8 tablespoons

Preparation:
8 minutes
Cooking:
11 minutes

• Preheat the oven to 180°C. Cook the **duck breasts** skin-side up for 6 minutes in a non-stick pan. Turn, empty out the fat and add the **rosemary**, **apricots**, **honey** and **soy sauce**.

• Return to the oven for 5 minutes, basting occasionally. Remove from the oven and leave to rest for 3 minutes.

• Cut the **duck breasts** in slices and serve with the **apricots** and the sauce.

DUCK LEGS WITH TURNIPS AND RADISHES

Tarragon
1 bunch

Baby turnips
x 12 (small)

Pink radishes
x 12

Olive oil
2 tablespoons

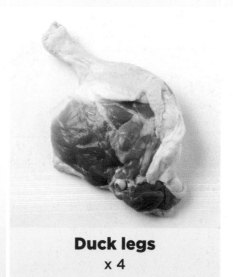

Duck legs
x 4

 **Salt, pepper**

**Preparation:
10 minutes
Cooking:
1 hour 5 minutes**

• Wash the **tarragon** and pick off the leaves. Wash, peel and remove the stalks from the **turnips** and **radishes**.
• Heat the **oil** in a casserole dish, brown the **duck legs** for 5 minutes, then add the **turnips** and **radishes**.
• Add 300 ml water, cover and simmer for 1 hour over a low heat. Add the **tarragon**, salt and pepper, mix in thoroughly and serve.

CHOPPED DUCK CONFIT WITH POTATOES

Duck confit
4 thighs

Potatoes
300 g

Sweet potatoes
300 g

Butter
80 g

Mixed salad
200 g

Walnut oil
2 tablespoons

 **Salt, pepper**

**Preparation:
15 minutes
Cooking:
1 hour**

• Preheat the oven to 170°C. Bake the **duck** for 30 minutes. Peel the **potatoes** and the **sweet potatoes** and add them to boiling, salted water. Cook for 20 minutes. Drain, and use a fork to mash the **potatoes** with the **butter**. Season with salt and pepper.

• Debone the **duck** and chop it up (with the skin on). Season the **salad** with the **walnut oil**. Serve the **duck** with the **salad** on top of the mashed **potatoes**.

TOMATOES STUFFED WITH DUCK

Tomatoes
x 12 (medium)

Duck confit
4 legs

Salt, pepper

Preparation:
20 minutes
Cooking:
35 minutes

• Preheat the oven to 180°C. Cut 'hats' off the **tomatoes** and scoop out the contents. Heat the **duck legs** for 10 minutes in a frying pan. Remove the skin and chop the meat and skin finely.

• Fill the **tomatoes** with the **duck** and place in a large oven dish. Bake in the oven for 25 minutes. Serve with mashed potato.

GUINEA FOWL WITH OLIVES

Tapenade
200 g

Guinea fowl
4 legs

 Salt, pepper

👤👤👤👤

🕐

**Preparation:
10 minutes
Cooking:
1 hour 10 minutes**

• Preheat the oven to 170°C. Mix the **tapenade** with 200 ml water and bring to the boil.
• Cut the **guinea fowl legs** in two, place in an oven dish, cover with the **tapenade** and cook in the oven for 1 hour, stirring occasionally.
• Serve with mashed potato.

GUINEA FOWL WITH CABBAGE

Savoy cabbage
x 1 (about 1 kg)

Guinea fowl
x 1 (cut in pieces)

Cooked streaky bacon
2 slices

Thyme
4 sprigs

Coarse salt
1 teaspoon

 Pepper

**Preparation:
10 minutes
Cooking:
1 hour 30 minutes**

• Wash the **cabbage** and cut into six. Place the pieces of **guinea fowl** and **cabbage** in a cast-iron casserole dish.
• Add the chopped **bacon, thyme, coarse salt** and a glass of water.
• Cover and simmer for 1 hour 30 minutes over a very low heat. Serve directly from the casserole dish.

TURKEY LEG WITH ONION FONDUE

Turkey leg
x 1

Spring onions
1 bunch

Maple syrup
6 tablespoons

Soy sauce
4 tablespoons

**Preparation:
10 minutes
Cooking: 1 hour**

• Preheat the oven to 180°C. Roast the **turkey leg** in an oven dish for 30 minutes.

• Peel the **spring onions**, slice thinly and arrange around the **turkey**. Cover with **maple syrup** and **soy sauce**.

• Cook for a further 30 minutes, basting regularly with the cooking juices. Serve with fresh pasta.

RABBIT WITH MUSTARD

Dijon mustard
4 tablespoons

Double cream
200 ml

Thyme
2 teaspoons

Rabbit legs
x 4

Garlic
8 cloves

Olive oil
2 tablespoons

 **Salt, pepper**

**Preparation:
5 minutes
Cooking:
45 minutes**

• Preheat the oven to 180°C. Beat the **mustard** together with the **cream** and **thyme**. Place the **rabbit legs** and the **garlic cloves** with the skin on in a large oven dish.

• Season with salt and pepper, drizzle with **olive oil** and bake in the oven for 20 minutes.

• Cover with the mustard cream and cook for a further 25 minutes. Remove from the oven and serve immediately.

COQ AU VIN STYLE CHICKEN WITH PRUNES

Chicken legs
x 4 (cut in two)

Lardons
300 g

Flour
1 tablespoon

Red wine
1 bottle (75 cl)

Prunes
x 10

  **Salt, pepper**

👤👤👤👤

🕐

**Preparation:
15 minutes
Cooking:
2 hours 10 minutes**

• Heat 3 tablespoons of oil in a casserole over high heat. Sear and brown the **chicken** and add the **lardons** and **flour**.

• Add the **red wine**, reduce the heat and simmer for 2 hours over a low heat, stirring occasionally.

• Add the **prunes**, season to taste and serve in the casserole dish.

ROLLED SOLE FILLETS WITH PESTO

Sole fillets
x 8

Pesto
1 tablespoon

 Salt, pepper

👤👤👤👤

🕐

Preparation:
5 minutes
Cooking:
35 minutes

• Preheat the oven to 170°C. Brush the **sole fillets** with **pesto**, roll up, place in an oven dish and bake for 35 minutes.
• Serve immediately with mashed potato or fresh pasta.

SKATE WITH TARRAGON

Tarragon
1 bunch

Skate wings
1.2 kg (whole, skin on)

  **Salt, pepper**

**Preparation:
10 minutes
Cooking:
20 minutes
Setting: 12 hours**

• Wash the **tarragon**, pick off the leaves and chop. Place the **skate** in a saucepan, cover with water and cook for 20 minutes over a low heat, then remove from the pan, reserving the cooking water.

• Remove the skin and cartilage. Mix the flesh with the **tarragon** and 50 ml cooking water. Transfer to a terrine, press down lightly and leave to draw in the refrigerator overnight. Serve in thick slices with a vinaigrette.

SEABASS CARPACCIO WITH RASPBERRIES

Tarragon
4 sprigs

Raspberries
x 20

Seabass fillets
500 g (skinless and boneless)

Lemons
x 2

Olive oil
4 tablespoons

 **Salt, pepper**

 👤👤👤👤

🕐
**Preparation:
10 minutes**

• Wash and chop the **tarragon**. Crush the **raspberries**. Cut the **seabass** into thin slices and arrange on 4 small plates.

• Add the **raspberries, tarragon, lemon juice** and **olive oil**, season with salt and pepper and serve with toast.

COD LOIN WITH TOMATO AND BASIL

Garlic
2 cloves

Tomatoes
x 4 (medium)

Basil
1 bunch

Olive oil
4 tablespoons

Cod loin steaks
x 4 (fresh or frozen)

Salt, pepper

Preparation:
10 minutes
Cooking:
20 minutes

• Preheat the oven to 170°C. Peel the **garlic**, dice the **tomatoes,** wash the **basil** and pick off the leaves.
• In a food processor, mix all of the above with 2 tablespoons **olive oil**, season with salt and pepper and set aside.
• Place the **cod** in an oven dish, drizzle with the remaining **olive oil** and bake in the oven for 20 minutes.
• Cover the **fish** with the cold sauce and serve.

BREAM IN SALT CRUST WITH HERBS

Rosemary
4 large sprigs

Thyme
10 sprigs

Flat-leaf parsley
½ bunch

Coarse grey salt
600 g

Bream
x 1 (1.5 kg, gutted)

**Preparation:
10 minutes
Cooking:
30 minutes**

• Preheat the oven to 170°C. Pick off the **herb** leaves and mix with the **coarse salt**.

• Place the **bream** on a baking sheet, cover with a thick layer of **salt** and bake in the oven for 30 minutes.

• Break up the **salt** crust, remove the skin and extract the fillets. Serve with a little olive oil.

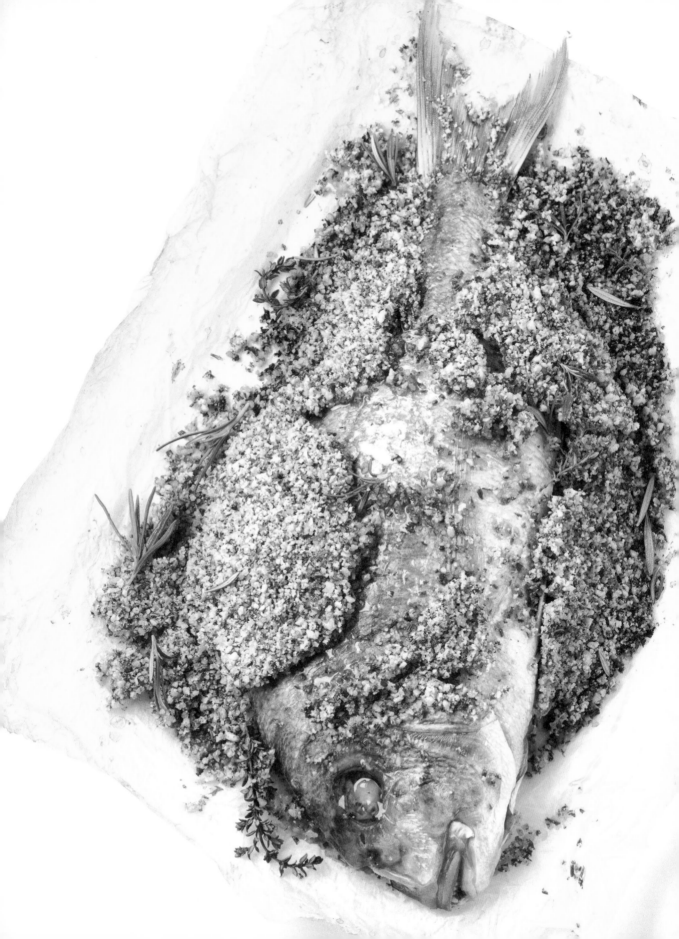

EXOTIC BREAM FILLETS

Tomatoes
x 4

Lemongrass
2 stems

Olive oil
4 tablespoons

Coconut milk
250 ml

Bream fillets
x 4 (skin on)

 **Salt, pepper**

**Preparation:
10 minutes
Cooking:
25 minutes**

• Preheat the oven to 180°C. Cut the **tomatoes** into cubes and the **lemongrass** into thin slices.

• Place the **tomatoes, lemongrass, olive oil** and **coconut milk** in an oven dish and bake for 15 minutes, stirring occasionally.

• Add the **bream fillets**, skin-side up, season with salt and pepper and cook for a further 10 minutes. Serve in the oven dish.

SEABASS TARTARE WITH MANGO

Mango
x 1

Seabass fillets
x 8 (skinless and boneless)

Coriander
1 bunch

Coconut milk
2 tablespoons

Olive oil
4 tablespoons

Lemon
x1 (2 tablespoons of juice)

 **Salt, pepper**

👤👤👤👤

🕐

**Preparation:
10 minutes**

• Peel the **mango** and cut in cubes.
• Cut the **seabass** into cubes. Wash and chop the **coriander**.
• Mix together the **seabass, mango, coriander, coconut milk, olive oil** and **lemon juice**. Season with salt and pepper and serve chilled with toast.

MONKFISH WITH CIDER AND HAM

Button mushrooms
300 g

Monkfish
800 g (skinless)

Air-dried ham
4 thin slices

Butter
50 g

Dry cider
250 ml

Double cream
250 ml

 **Salt, pepper**

👤👤👤👤

**Preparation:
15 minutes
Cooking:
30 minutes**

• Wash the **mushrooms** and slice them thinly. Wrap the **monkfish** in the **ham** and tie with string.
• Heat the **butter** in a casserole dish, sear the **fish** and the **mushrooms**, then set the **fish** aside on a plate.
• Add the **cider** to the pan, reduce to three-quarters, add the **cream** and cook for 5 minutes over a high heat.
• Add the **fish** and cook for a further 20 minutes.

MONKFISH CHEEKS WITH MUSHROOMS

Dried porcini mushrooms
40 g

Monkfish cheeks
x 12

Butter
50 g

Soy sauce
2 tablespoons

Double cream
500 ml

Hazelnut oil
2 tablespoons

  Salt, pepper

**Preparation:
5 minutes
Soaking: 30 minutes
Cooking: 25 minutes**

• Soak the **mushrooms** for 30 minutes in 300 ml water, remove from the water and cut into pieces. Reduce the soaking water to half.

• In a casserole dish, sear the **monkfish cheeks** in the **butter** for 5 minutes, add the mushroom water and **soy sauce**, reduce by half and add the **cream** and **mushrooms**. Cook for 10 minutes over a low heat and drizzle with **hazelnut oil** before serving.

MACKEREL WITH MUSTARD AND THYME

Mackerel fillets
x 4 (skin on but boneless)

Dijon mustard
4 tablespoons

Thyme
1 teaspoon

 **Salt, pepper**

**Preparation:
5 minutes
Cooking:
25 minutes**

• Preheat the oven to 170°C. Arrange the **mackerel** on a baking sheet, brush with **mustard**, season with salt and pepper and sprinkle with **thyme**.
• Bake in the oven for 25 minutes until the **mackerel** are well-cooked and crispy.

RED MULLET WITH MANDARIN JUICE

Mandarin oranges
x 8

Soy sauce
2 tablespoons

Olive oil
4 tablespoons

Red mullet fillets
x 8 (fresh or frozen)

  **Salt, pepper**

**Preparation:
10 minutes
Cooking:
5 minutes**

• Preheat the oven to 180°C. Squeeze the **mandarins** and mix the juice with the **soy sauce** and **olive oil**.
• Place the **mullet fillets** in an oven dish and bake for 5 minutes.
• Transfer to a deep plate, cover with the **mandarin** juice and serve.

OVEN-BAKED FISH WITH TOMATOES

Tomatoes
x 2

Hairtail fillets
500 g

Olive oil
4 tablespoons

White wine
50 ml

Thyme
1 teaspoon

Bay leaves
x 2

Salt, pepper

**Preparation:
10 minutes
Cooking:
30 minutes**

• Preheat the oven to 170°C. Wash the **tomatoes** and cut into rounds. Cut the **hairtail fillets** into small pieces.
• Arrange overlapping rows of **tomatoes** and **fish** in a gratin dish. Season with salt and pepper, add the **olive oil**, **white wine**, **thyme** and **bay leaves** and bake in the oven for 30 minutes. Eat very hot, accompanied by rice.

COURGETTE AND HADDOCK GRATIN

Courgettes
x 3

Haddock
400 g (skinless)

Basil
20 leaves

Parmesan shavings
200 g

Olive oil
4 tablespoons

Preparation:
10 minutes
Cooking:
35 minutes

• Preheat the oven to 170°C. Wash the **courgettes**, remove the stems and cut lengthways into thin strips using a vegetable peeler.

• Cut the **haddock** into thin slices. Wash and chop the **basil**.

• Fill a gratin dish with layers of **courgettes**, **Parmesan**, **haddock**, **basil** and **olive oil**. Bake in the oven for 35 minutes and serve.

MARINATED SALMON WITH ANISEED

Salmon fillets
600 g (skinless)

Coarse grey salt
2 tablespoons

Sugar
2 tablespoons

Dill
1 bunch

Aniseed
2 teaspoons

Olive oil
2 tablespoons

 **Salt, pepper**

**Preparation:
10 minutes
Marinating:
12 hours**

• Place the **salmon** in a container, cover with **salt**, **sugar** and three-quarters of the **dill**. Cover the container with kitchen film and marinate for 12 hours in the refrigerator.
• Remove the **salmon** from the marinade, cut into thin slices and serve covered with chopped **dill**, **aniseed** and **olive oil**.

SALMON TARTARE WITH ASPARAGUS

Green asparagus
x 8 stems

Salmon fillets
500 g (skinless)

Lemons
x 3

Olive oil
4 tablespoons

  Salt, pepper

**Preparation:
10 minutes
Cooking: 1 minutes
Setting: 5 minutes**

• Peel and trim the **asparagus** and blanch for 1 minute. Rinse in cold water and cut into small pieces.
• Cut the **salmon** into small cubes and mix with the **asparagus**. Add the juice of the **lemons** and the **olive oil**.
• Season with salt and pepper, leave to rest in the refrigerator for 5 minutes and serve with toast.

BAKED JOHN DORY WITH LEMON SAUCE

Coriander
1 bunch

Preserved lemons
x 2

Olive oil
6 tablespoons

Pomegranate seeds
50 g

Soy sauce
2 tablespoons

John Dory fish
x 1 (1.6 kg, gutted)

 Pepper

👤👤👤👤

🕐
**Preparation:
10 minutes
Cooking:
25 minutes**

• Preheat the oven to 170°C. Wash and chop the **coriander**. Chop the peel of the **preserved lemons**.
• Mix all the above ingredients with the **olive oil**, **pomegranate seeds** and **soy sauce** and set aside.
• Bake the **John Dory** in a large oven dish for 25 minutes. Season with pepper and serve the **fish** hot, covered with the sauce and accompanied by a salad.

TUNA CARPACCIO WITH CORIANDER

Coriander
1 bunch

Olive oil
4 tablespoons

Soy sauce
2 tablespoons

Lime
x 1

Tuna
500 g

 Pepper

👤👤👤👤

🕐
**Preparation:
10 minutes**

• Wash the **coriander** and pick off the leaves. Mix the **olive oil** with the **soy sauce** and the juice of the **lime**.
• Cut the **tuna** into thin slices and arrange on 4 plates.
• Pour the dressing over the **fish**, sprinkle with **coriander**, season with pepper and serve with toast.

TUNA TARTARE WITH TARAMASALATA

Lemons
x 2

Tuna steak
500 g

Chives
1 bunch

Taramasalata
2 tablespoons

Olive oil
2 tablespoons

 **Salt, pepper**

**Preparation:
10 minutes**

• Squeeze the **lemons**. Cut the **tuna** into small cubes.
• Chop the **chives** and mix with the **tuna**, the juice of the **lemons**, **taramasalata** and **oil**.
• Season with salt and pepper, and transfer to individual plates. Serve with slices of toast.

TUNA IN OIL AND PEPPERS

Red peppers
x 2

Green pepper
x 1

Tuna in oil
2 tins

 Salt, pepper

Preparation:
10 minutes
Cooking:
25 minutes

- Wash the **peppers**, remove the stalks and seeds and slice thinly.
- Sear the **peppers** in a casserole dish with the oil from the **tuna**, and fry gently for 25 minutes over a low heat.
- Turn off the heat, season with salt and pepper and add the **tuna**.
- Mix together and serve with fresh pasta.

TUNA CUBES IN A SESAME MARINADE

Tuna steak
500 g (red or white)

Limes
x 2

Sesame oil
3 tablespoons

Sesame seeds
1 tablespoon

Soy sauce
6 tablespoons

**Preparation:
10 minutes
Marinating:
10 minutes**

• Cut the **tuna** into cubes and mix with the juice of the **limes**, **sesame oil**, **sesame seeds** and **soy sauce**.
• Marinate in the refrigerator for 10 minutes, stirring occasionally, and serve with toasted farmhouse bread.

FRICASSEE OF SQUID WITH BASIL

Garlic
2 cloves

Olive oil
4 tablespoons

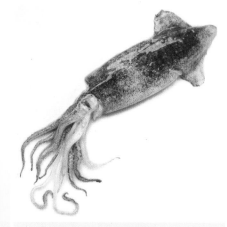

Squid
800 g (skinned and gutted)

White wine
1 glass (150 ml)

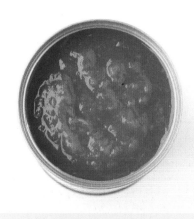

Chopped tomatoes
1 tin (400 g)

Basil
20 leaves

 **Salt, pepper**

🕐

**Preparation:
10 minutes
Cooking:
45 minutes**

• Peel and chop the **garlic**. Heat the **olive oil** in a casserole dish and sear the **squid** and **garlic**.
• Brown for 5 minutes, add the **white wine**, reduce and add the **tomatoes**.
• Season with salt and pepper and simmer for 40 minutes over low heat.
• Add the **basil** leaves and mix well.

STUFFED SQUID

Squid
x 8 (skinned and gutted)

Sausage meat
250 g

Egg
x 1

Dried thyme
1 tablespoon

Tomato purée
500 ml

White wine
250 ml

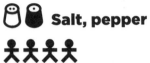 **Salt, pepper**

👥👥👥👥

🕐

**Preparation:
10 minutes
Cooking: 1 hour**

• Preheat the oven to 170°C. Cut up the **squid** tentacles and mix with the **sausage meat**, **egg** and **thyme**. Season with salt and pepper and knead together.
• Stuff the **squid** and close with a wooden cocktail stick.
• Place in an oven dish, cover with **tomato purée** and **white wine** and bake in the oven for 1 hour, basting occasionally.

OCTOPUS CASSEROLE

Red onions
x 2

Olive oil
4 tablespoons

Octopus
1.2 kg

Red wine
1 bottle (75 cl)

Chopped tomatoes
2 tins (800 g)

Thyme
4 sprigs

Salt, pepper

**Preparation:
10 minutes
Cooking: 1 hour**

• Peel the **onions** and slice thinly.
• Cut the **octopus** into pieces. Heat the **oil** in a casserole dish, lightly brown the **onions** and **octopus** and add the **wine, tomatoes** and **thyme**.
• Simmer for 1 hour over a low heat, stirring regularly. Serve very hot accompanied by fresh pasta.

CUTTLEFISH WITH INK

Garlic
4 cloves

Olive oil
4 tablespoons

Cuttlefish fillets
600 g

White wine
1 glass (150 ml)

Cuttlefish ink
4 sachets

Thyme
4 sprigs

 **Salt, pepper**

Preparation:
5 minutes
Cooking:
30 minutes

• Peel and chop the **garlic**. Heat the **oil** in a casserole dish and sear the **cuttlefish** and **garlic** for 5 minutes.
• Add the **white wine**, reduce to half and add the **ink**, **thyme** and a glass of water.
• Simmer for 25 minutes over a very low heat, season with salt and pepper, and serve with rice.

PRAWN CEVICHE WITH LIME

Limes
x 4

Coriander
1 bunch

Prawns
x 8 (large)

Olive oil
6 tablespoons

  Salt, pepper

**Preparation:
15 minutes
Marinating:
15 minutes**

• Squeeze the **limes**. Wash the **coriander** and pick off and chop the leaves.
• Peel the **prawns** and marinate in a dish for 15 minutes with the **olive oil, lime** juice and **coriander**.
• Season with salt and pepper and serve with slices of toast.

KING PRAWN CURRY

Prawns
x 8 (large)

Olive oil
2 tablespoons

Basil
40 leaves

Coconut milk
1 litre

Curry powder
2 tablespoons

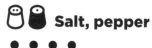 **Salt, pepper**

**Preparation:
15 minutes
Cooking:
20 minutes**

• Preheat the oven to 180°C. Peel the bodies of the **prawns**, retaining the heads and tails, and place in an oven dish.

• Mix the **coconut milk** with the **curry powder** and add to the **prawns** with the **olive oil** and **basil**, season with salt and pepper and bake for 20 minutes.

• Serve in the oven dish, accompanied by either rice or fresh pasta.

KING PRAWNS WITH VANILLA BUTTER

Vanilla
4 pods

Soft butter
120 g

Prawns
8 (large)

 Salt, pepper

**Preparation:
8 minutes
Cooking:
8 minutes**

• Split open the **vanilla pods**, scrape out the contents and mix the seeds with the **butter**.

• Cut the **prawns** in two and sear in the **butter**, cut the **vanilla pods** into pieces, add to the pan and fry for 6 to 8 minutes over a low heat, stirring continuously.

• Season well with salt and pepper and serve with mashed potato.

LOBSTERS WITH CREAM

Lobsters
x 2 (800 g each)

Butter
80 g

Cognac
50 ml

Double cream
500 ml

Tomato paste
2 teaspoons

  Salt, pepper

Preparation:
40 minutes
Cooking: 35 minutes
Setting: 30 minutes

• Plunge the **lobsters** in boiling water for 1 minute.
• Heat the **butter** in a casserole and brown the **lobsters** in the hot **butter** for 10 minutes.
• Deglaze and flambé with the **cognac**, then add the **cream** and **tomato paste**.
• Beat and cook for 20 minutes over low heat.
• Turn off the heat, return the **lobsters** to the casserole, leave to draw for 30 minutes, then reheat and serve.

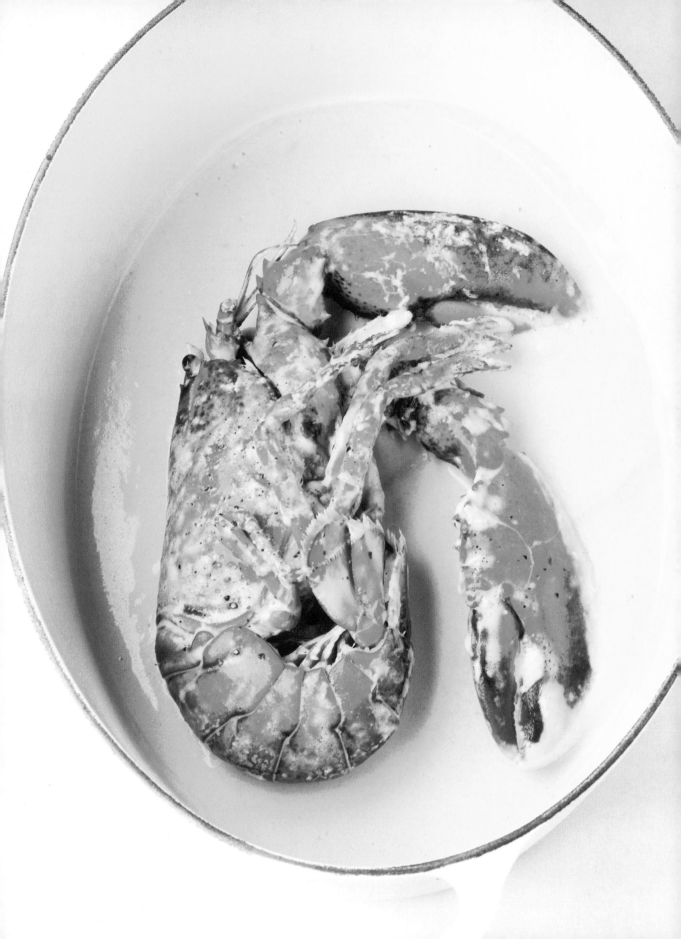

HOT OYSTERS WITH GINGER

Flat oysters
x 8 (large)

Double cream
1 tablespoon

Butter
80 g

Fresh ginger
30 g

Lime
x 1

Salmon caviar
2 tablespoons

 **Salt, pepper**

**Preparation:
20 minutes
Cooking:
5 minutes**

• Open the **oysters**, pouring any seawater from them into a saucepan. Remove from the shells and poach for 2 seconds in their water. Remove from the water and replace in their shells.

• Heat the **cream** in a saucepan, then remove from the heat, add the **butter** in pieces and beat together with the **cream**. Grate the **ginger** and squeeze the **lime**. Add the **ginger**, **lime juice** and **salmon caviar** to the **cream** and pour over the **oysters**.

322

POMEGRANATE AND CORIANDER OYSTERS

Pomegranate
x 1

Coriander
1 bunch

Limes
x 3

Soy sauce
6 tablespoons

Olive oil
4 tablespoons

Flat oysters
x 24

**Preparation:
20 minutes**

• Peel the **pomegranate** and collect the seeds. Wash and chop the **coriander**. Squeeze the **limes**.
• Mix all the ingredients in a large bowl.
• Open the **oysters**, arrange on individual plates, cover with the dressing, leave to rest for 3 minutes and enjoy.

MOULES MARINIÈRE WITH CURRY

Mussels
2 litres

Double cream
330 ml

Thyme
4 sprigs

Curry powder
1 tablespoon

 **Salt, pepper**

👤👤👤👤

🕐

**Preparation:
10 minutes
Cooking:
5 minutes**

• Scrape and wash the **mussels**, tip into a casserole dish and add the **cream**, **thyme** and **curry powder**.
• Bring to the boil and cook for 5 minutes over high heat, stirring continuously.
• When the **mussels** open, turn off the heat, stir thoroughly and serve.

CLAMS WITH COCONUT MILK

Lemongrass
2 stems

Coconut milk
500 ml

Thyme
2 sprigs

Clams
x 24

Salt, pepper

👤👤👤👤

**Preparation:
10 minutes
Cooking:
10 minutes**

• Peel the **lemongrass** and slice thinly.
• Pour the **coconut milk** into a saucepan with the **lemongrass**, **thyme** and **clams**.
• Bring to the boil, stirring continuously, and turn off the heat when the **clams** open. Serve in 4 individual bowls.

SCALLOP CARPACCIO WITH PASSION FRUIT

Passion fruit
x 3

Olive oil
4 tablespoons

Scallops without coral
x 12 (fresh or frozen)

  Salt, pepper

Preparation:
10 minutes
Marinating:
5 minutes

• Cut the **passion fruit** in two, collect the flesh and the juice and mix with the **olive oil**.
• Cut the **scallops** in thin slices and arrange in rosettes on 4 plates.
• Brush with the **passion fruit** oil.
• Season with salt and pepper, leave to draw for 5 minutes and serve.

SCALLOPS WITH HERB GAZPACHO

Basil
20 leaves

Dill
1 bunch

Scallops
x 12 (fresh or frozen)

Olive oil
6 tablespoons

Gazpacho
1 litre

 **Salt, pepper**

👤👤👤👤

🕐

**Preparation:
15 minutes
Cooking:
2 minutes**

• Wash the **basil** and **dill** and chop coarsely. In a frying pan, brown the **scallops**, with or without the coral, for 2 minutes in half the **olive oil**.

• Fill 4 deep plates with **gazpacho**, add the **scallops** and **herbs**, season with salt and pepper, add the remaining **olive oil** and serve.

DESERT ROSES

Milk chocolate
200 g

Corn flakes
130 g

**Preparation:
15 minutes
Refrigeration:
1 hour**

• Melt the **chocolate** in a bain-marie, add the **corn flakes** and mix together.
• Form into small, even-sized heaps on a large baking sheet. Leave to set in the refrigerator for 1 hour and enjoy cold.

NUTELLA® FONDANT MOUSSE

Eggs
x 4

Nutella®
250 g

👤👤👤👤

🕐
Preparation:
10 minutes
Cooking:
5 minutes

• Preheat the oven to 180°C. Beat the **eggs** in a large bowl for 8 minutes using an electric mixer.
• Soften the **Nutella**® in the microwave and fold gently into the beaten **eggs** with a spatula. Spoon into 4 ramekins and bake in the oven for 5 minutes. Serve hot with a scoop of vanilla ice cream.

COCONUT ROCKS

Egg whites
x 2

Sugar
80 g

Grated coconut
180 g

Preparation:
10 minutes
Cooking:
5 minutes

• Preheat the oven to 210°C. Using the tips of your fingers, mix the **egg whites** with the **sugar** and the **coconut**.
• Form into small pyramids and arrange on a baking sheet lined with baking paper without pressing down. Bake in the oven for 5 minutes, leave to cool and enjoy.

CHERRY AND PISTACHIO COOKIES

Glacé cherries
100 g

Shelled pistachios
50 g

Butter
100 g (soft)

Sugar
50 g

Flour
100 g

Preparation:
15 minutes
Cooking:
10 minutes
Refrigeration: 1 hour

• Chop the **cherries** and **pistachios**.
• Mix together the **butter**, **sugar**, **flour**, **cherries** and **pistachios**.
• Form the mixture into a sausage shape and refrigerate for 1 hour. Preheat the oven to 180°C.
• Cut the sausage into even-sized biscuits 1 cm thick. Arrange on a baking sheet and bake for 10 minutes. Leave to cool.

PASSION FRUIT PROFITEROLES

Dark chocolate
200 g

Double cream
200 ml

Small choux pastries
x 12

Passion fruit sorbet
300 g

**Preparation:
15 minutes**

• In a large bowl, chop the **chocolate** with a large knife. Bring the **cream** to the boil and pour over the **chocolate**, beating it so that it melts.

• Set aside in a bain-marie.

• Fill the **choux pastries** with the **sorbet**, arrange on individual plates, top with the hot **chocolate** and serve.

WHIPPED CREAM WITH RASPBERRIES

Whipping cream
600 ml

Icing sugar
1 tablespoon

Raspberries
400 g

Preparation:
10 minutes
Refrigeration:
10 minutes

• In a well-chilled bowl, whip the **cream** with an electric whisk, add the **sugar** and **raspberries**, continue whisking for 2 minutes, then spoon into glass dishes.
• Refrigerate for 10 minutes and serve.

SMOOTH CREAM WITH WILD STRAWBERRIES

Mascarpone
250 g

Whipping cream
330 ml

Icing sugar
1 tablespoon

Wild strawberries
400 g

Preparation:
10 minutes
Refrigeration: 1 hour

• Mix together the **mascarpone**, **cream** and **sugar** in a mixer bowl and refrigerate for 1 hour. 5 minutes before serving, beat the mixture to a smooth whipped cream.
• Serve in glass dishes with the **wild strawberries**.

APPLE AND CINNAMON PUFF

Apples
x 4

Butter
50 g

Cinnamon
2 teaspoons

Puff pastry
x 1 sheet

Sugar
4 tablespoons

Preparation:
10 minutes
Cooking:
25 minutes

• Peel the **apples** and cut into cubes. Fry lightly for 5 minutes in a pan with the **butter** and **cinnamon** and leave to cool.

• Preheat the oven to 180°C. Spread out the pastry on a baking sheet, cover with **apples**, sprinkle with 3 tablespoons of **sugar**, fold over the pastry and close.

• Sprinkle the remaining **sugar** over the top and bake for 25 minutes. Serve hot or cold.

STRAWBERRIES IN A WINE AND MINT SYRUP

Red wine
200 ml

Sugar
15 cubes

Star anise
x 2

Cinnamon
2 sticks

Mint
1 bunch

Strawberries
2 punnets

Preparation:
10 minutes
Cooking:
25 minutes
Refrigeration: 3 hours

- Simmer the **wine** with the **sugar** and **spices** over a low heat for 25 minutes.
- Wash the **mint**. Wash the **strawberries** and cut into small pieces.
- Turn off the heat under the syrup. Add the entire bunch of **mint**, cover and leave to draw for 3 hours in the refrigerator.
- Remove the bunch of **mint**, add the **strawberries** and serve.

WATERMELON WITH LEMON SYRUP

Lemons
x 2

Icing sugar
2 tablespoons

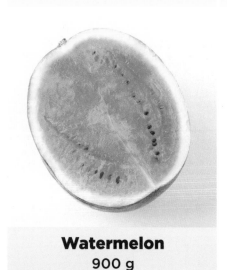

Watermelon
900 g

**Preparation:
10 minutes
Cooking:
25 minutes**

• Grate the peel of the **lemons** and squeeze out the juice. Put the juice and peel in a saucepan, add 1 glass of water (about 50 ml) and the **sugar**.
• Cook gently for 25 minutes over a low heat and leave to cool.
• Peel the **watermelon** and cut the flesh into cubes. Mix the **melon** with the lemon syrup and serve well-chilled.

POACHED PEARS WITH WINE AND SAFFRON

Pears
x 4 (large) or x 8 (small)

Sweet wine
1 bottle (75 cl)

Saffron
10 threads

Gingerbread
2 slices

**Preparation:
15 minutes
Cooking:
45 minutes
Refrigeration: 1 hour**

• Peel the **pears**, retaining the cores and stalks. Place in a saucepan with the **wine** and **saffron**.
• Cook over low heat for 45 minutes. Turn off the heat and leave to cool in the syrup for an hour.
• Arrange the cold **pears** in deep plates, add the **syrup** and crumble the **gingerbread** over them.

STRAWBERRY AND BASIL SALAD

Strawberries
400 g

Icing sugar
1 tablespoon

Lemons
x 2

Basil
10 leaves

Olive oil
2 tablespoons

**Preparation:
10 minutes
Refrigeration:
15 minutes**

• Wash and hull the **strawberries** and cut into pieces. Squeeze the **lemons** and mix the juice with the **sugar** and **strawberries** in a salad bowl.
• Refrigerate for 15 minutes, add the chopped **basil** and **olive oil**, mix together and serve.

WHIPPED CREAM WITH BLUEBERRIES

Whipping cream
600 ml

Bitter cocoa powder
2 tablespoons

Icing sugar
2 teaspoons

Blueberries
400 g

**Preparation:
15 minutes
Refrigeration: 1 hour**

• Pour the **cream** into a bowl and refrigerate for 1 hour. 5 minutes before serving, beat the cream until smooth, add the **cocoa** and **sugar** and beat for a further 1 minute to mix well.

• Serve in ramekins with the **blueberries**.

CONTENTS

INDEX

HAIRTAIL FISH
Oven baked fish with tomatoes
288-9

HAM
Baked asparagus with ham 19
Chicory with country ham 218-19
Courgette & ham pizza with pesto
116-17
Gazpacho with asparagus 30
Ham, dandelion & pear pizzas 114-15
Macaroni cheese with ham 80-1
Monkfish with cider & ham 280-1
Mozzarella & fig skewers 154-5
Quail with grapes 246-7

HAY
Pork knuckle in hay 207

HAZELNUT
Cream of pumpkin soup with
hazelnuts 40-1
Hazelnut & radicchio farfalle 74-5

HONEY
Apricot & rosemary duck breasts
252-3
Caramelised pork 212-13
Chicken with cashew nuts 230-1
Honey-glazed turnips 139
Pork ribs with BBQ sauce 208-9

J

JOHN DORY
Baked John Dory with lemon sauce
296-7

K

KETCHUP
Fresh beef tartare 202
Pork ribs with BBQ sauce 208-9
Potato wedges with salt & rosemary
140-1
Savoury meat balls 192

KIDNEY
Veal kidneys with mustard sauce
172-3

KIDNEY BEANS
Chilli con carne 196-7

L

LAMB
7-hour leg of lamb 168-9

Lamb with potatoes 162-3
Lamb skewers with mango 164-5
Navarin of lamb with vegetables
160-1
Slow-roasted shoulder of lamb 166-7

LARDONS
Beef bourguignon 188-9
Coq au vin style chicken with prunes
266-7
Gouda & cumin seed tartiflette 146-7

LEEK
Leek gratin with Reblochon cheese
158
Leek & Parmesan tart 120-1

LEMON
Baked John Dory with lemon sauce
296-7
Button mushroom pizzas 106-7
Chicken with coconut & lemongrass
232-3
Chicken with parsley & Parmesan
240-1
Fried chicken with avocado cream
234-5
Mini sausage pizzas 10-11
Ricotta & pea spread 14-15
Roast chicken with paprika 236-7
Salmon tartare with asparagus
294-5
Seabass carpaccio with raspberries
270-1
Smoked salmon with whipped cream
12-13
Strawberry & basil salad 354-5
Sweet potato chips 142-3
Tuna tartare with taramasalata 300-1
Watermelon with lemon syrup 350-1

LEMONGRASS
Chicken with coconut & lemongrass
232-3
Clams with coconut milk 328-9
Exotic bream fillets 276-7

LENTILS
Lentil, salmon & tarragon salad 62-3

LETTUCE
Roquefort salad 70-1

LIME
Pomegranate & coriander oysters
324-5
Prawn ceviche with lime 314-15
Thai salad 68-9
Tuna cubes in sesame marinade
304-5

LIVER
Chicken liver salad with apricots
72-3
Poultry liver terrine 26-7

LOBSTER
Lobsters with cream 320-1

MACARONI see **PASTA**

MACKEREL
Mackerel with mustard & thyme
284-5

MANDARIN ORANGES
Fusilli with sardines 78
Red mullet with mandarin juice
286-7

MANGE-TOUT PEAS
Navarin of lamb with vegetables 160

MANGO
Lamb skewers with mango 164-5
Seabass tartare with mango 278-9

MASCARPONE
Smooth cream with wild strawberries
344-5

MAYONNAISE
Roast rib of beef with false Béarnaise
198-9

MELON
Melon with smoked salmon & mint
56-7
Melon, tomato & basil salad 58-9

MINT
Cold ratatouille with mint 128-9
Courgette fritters in a salad 136-7
Lamb skewers with mango 164-5
Melon with smoked salmon & mint
56-7
Strawberries in a wine & mint syrup
348-9
Tabbouleh with salmon & radishes
64-5

MONKFISH
Monkfish cheeks with mushrooms
282-3
Monkfish with cider & ham 280-1

MOREL see **MUSHROOMS**

MOZZARELLA
Aubergine gratin 132-3
Mozzarella & fig skewers 154-5

MUSHROOMS
Beef bourguignon 188-9
Blanquette of veal with asparagus
170-1

An Hachette UK Company
www.hachette.co.uk

First published in Great Britain in 2016 by Hamlyn, a division of
Octopus Publishing Group Ltd
Carmelite House
50 Victoria Embankment
London EC4Y 0DZ
www.octopusbooks.co.uk

First published in France in 2015 by Hachette Livre (Hachette
Pratique)
www.hachette-pratique.com
Copyright © Hachette Livre (Hachette Pratique) 2015

English translation copyright © Octopus Publishing Group Ltd 2016

ISBN 978-0-60063-422-5

A CIP catalogue record for this book is available from the British
Library.

Printed and bound in Spain

10 9 8 7 6 5 4 3 2

Director: Catherine Saunier-Talec
Artistic director: Antoine Béon
Editorial director: Céline Le Lamer

Packager: Édiclic
Editorial co-ordinator: Delphine Blétry and Séverine Charbonnel
Graphic design and layout: Marie-Paule Jaulme
Production: Amélie Latsch
Partnerships manager: Sophie Morier (smorier@hachette-livre.fr)

UK edition
Editor: Phoebe Morgan
Translation: Rae Walter, in association with First Edition
Translations Ltd, Cambridge, UK.